# Make It a Life
## *Worth Living*

### YOUR PURPOSE, HEALTH, AND LEGACY

## Barry E. Moschel

For information about this title, contact the publisher:
Make It A Life Worth Living, LLC.
www.makeitalifeworthliving.com
barry@makeitalifeworthliving.com

ISBN: 979-8-9908730-0-1 (hardcover)
ISBN: 979-8-9908730-1-8 (softcover)
ISBN: 979-8-9908730-2-5 (eBook)

Printed in the United States of America
Cover and Interior design: 1106 Design

*Dedicated to your infinite possibilities.*
*May you find your best path forward for living your best life.*

# Giving Back

*As you grow older, you will discover that you have two hands,*
*one for helping yourself, the other for helping others.*
(Audrey Hepburn)

# My Mission

My mission is to share some simple lessons on how to live a good life while donating a significant portion of the profits from the sale of this book to solid, well-known charitable organizations. My hope is to promote the concept that having purpose, maximizing health, aging gracefully, and having a deliberate eye toward legacy planning will lead to an enriched and more fulfilling life: a life worth living.

# Table of Contents

# What Makes It a Life Worth Living?

Simply reflecting on this question can provide a spark that leads to a more fulfilling life.

In *Make It a Life Worth Living*, author Barry Moschel does more than simply reflect on this important topic. After spending many years seeking to understand what makes people more content and satisfied with life, Moschel believes he has the answers. These answers have so enhanced his life, he wants to share them with others.

After working on his project for many years, he gave me an early draft of this book. As one who has also spent years seeking keys to a more fulfilling life, his book blew me away.

Among the many inspirational takeaways is his chapter on our purpose: on why we live. For example, he describes the difference between purpose and mission:

> *Your purpose is why you do something while your mission is what you do. When you have purpose, you have focus, which drives your passion. Life is challenging, yet more fun and interesting because finding purpose will influence your behavior, goals, motivation, lifestyle choices, and actions.*

He quotes Matthew Kelly on the importance of purpose:

> *If there is purpose and meaning to our lives, then the highest levels of living must be linked to discovering that meaning and fulfilling that purpose. It stands to reason then that there*

*should be a relationship between the purpose and meaning of life and our dreams.*

But what is our purpose and how can we find it? He provides Dan Buettner's thoughtful and incisive answer:

*Articulating your personal mission statement can be a good start. Begin by answering this question in a single, memorable sentence: Why do you get up in the morning? Consider what you're passionate about, how you enjoy using your talents, and what is truly important to you.*

Buettner's advice led me to one of the many opportunities this book provides for introspection, conversation, and growth. Why do I get up in the morning? Taking Buettner's advice I spent several productive hours putting my purpose into a single memorable and impactful sentence. I have often been excited about getting up in the morning, but clearly articulating my purpose made it even more exciting than it had been.

Unfortunately, too many of us fail to think about our purpose. Some don't believe they have a purpose. They simply get up and routinely go through the motions of living. Without purpose, it can be more difficult to get up in the morning, and more difficult to have a life worth living.

Moschel's book has inspired a number of productive conversations about purpose. For example, my wife didn't think she had a purpose. She was wrong. As we talked about it, it became clear her purpose was so instinctive she never thought of it. As a loving person who consistently provides emotional support for family and friends, she has never hesitated to help anyone in need, including perfect strangers. After talking it over, her purpose became clear—it was to comfort and help others with her wise counsel, empathy, and love.

While purpose may be the most important element, it is only the beginning of the formula for achieving a life worth living. In another impactful chapter the importance of being present is discussed. Life occurs from moment to moment; to fully enjoy life we have to be fully engaged at each moment. This means providing our full attention to those we are conversing with, appreciating each wonder of nature before us, and acknowledging each precious moment spent with those we love.

There are a number of chapters on the importance of maintaining a healthy life, both physically and emotionally. In today's hectic world, emotional stress has the potential to dominate our lives, creating barriers to both our physical health and to a more fulfilling life. Chapters on exercise, love, faith and religion, breathing, meditating, friends, family, humor, tragedy and death, and celebrating victories and milestones are all important in dealing effectively with the challenges life often throws our way.

Additionally, there is a section dedicated to legacy planning and the importance of living a life with distinction and grace. Leading by example, being charitable, and having authentic moral values and priceless traditions that can be passed on and shared by future generations are ways to memorialize our life while further enhancing our purpose. True wealth or happiness is not always measured around material possessions, status, and money but more a reflection on how to live our best life while simultaneously impacting and helping others, thus making a positive difference in the world around us.

Moschel's insights benefit from his extensive use of quotes from writers, poets, religious figures, celebrities, politicians, and captains of industry. He weaves their advice and wisdom in a way that provides the depth and detail necessary to help achieve a more meaningful and productive life.

The wisdom in this book has enhanced my life and will enhance the lives of many others. I plan to give the book to my children, their children, and anyone else who is interested in benefiting from the keys to making theirs a life worth living.

*Dr. Robert Genetski is one of the nation's leading economists. He is a teacher, columnist, public speaker, consultant, and author. His books include* Rich Nation, Poor Nation, Classical Economic Principles & The Wealth of Nations, *and* Is There Evidence of God?: An Economist Searches for Answers.

# Introduction

*The good life is a process, not a state of being. It is a direction,*
*not a destination.* (Carl Rogers)

Don't we all want the same thing? To live a healthy and fulfilling life. One that we enjoy, that brings happiness, laughter, and peace to ourselves and those around us. A life of meaning and purpose, being able to age gracefully, while leaving a meaningful legacy for future generations. A legacy that is not just measured by wealth but also by values and life lessons left behind, such as lessons of love, compassion, and kindness. We want to be remembered fondly for something we have accomplished, someone we have helped, or in some measurable capacity, making a positive impact on society in the time we have had living in this world.

As we age we may realize that life is complicated and goes by quickly. To quote Ferris Bueller from the movie *Ferris Bueller's Day Off*: "Life moves pretty fast. If you don't stop and look around once in a while, you could miss it."

This book presents an upbeat integrated approach about how to live your best life. It has important, practical, and common-sense concepts that you may already know but could use a refresher course on. Let me explain why I wrote this book and the road it took to get there.

My day job for many decades has been as an independent financial advisor. I help people with their short- and long-term goals, managing investments through various risk factors and economic environments. Part of my job is helping people plan for retirement and legacy from a monetary standpoint. For some time I noticed that many in our industry, myself included, were not covering what I perceived was a missing gap of nonmonetary matters related to purpose, health, and legacy, areas that enable people to live inspired and fulfilling lives. From my viewpoint, it became increasingly apparent that there are many people looking to find purpose and meaning in their lives, whether they realize it or not, at all ages, but particularly for those near or in retirement. I continued to focus on my normal busy daily routines at work because I did not have the capacity to figure out how to help in those areas.

Several events occurred that eventually made me circle back to this topic. The first was when my mother passed away in 2016. I had already lost my father four years earlier. It was a gut punch as I felt that I lost a part of me and a generation of love and traditions. Then a few years later I saw what the beginning of Covid brought to the psychology of an entire planet. There was pervasive fear everywhere as people were paralyzed from living their normal lives. I had witnessed panic, misery, and gloom before but never on such a massive global level as during 2020 and 2021.

This gave me time to pause and reflect on my own life and mortality. What could I learn from the world around me and how could I grow from it? What was my purpose? How could I stay healthy, both mentally and physically, through all this heightened anxiety and disorder? What kind of legacy did I want to leave to the world? How could I live my best life and rise above all this chaos? I remembered the missing gap of nonmonetary matters related to purpose, health, and legacy and ideas started to form in my mind. While I was wrapping up my first book on retirement income planning, I started reading and researching for answers to the questions and the connections I was looking for. I found a slew of informative authors and mentors to help teach and show me the way. I also went back to school virtually and received a designation on philanthropy to enhance my education. All this new knowledge inspired and excited me. It provided me the purpose I was seeking. I organized my research while simultaneously collecting an extensive supply of quotes to supplement the rest of the content I was accumulating. I started the framework and the outline of this book and then began writing in early 2023. The process of writing and editing several drafts, with feedback from others I trust and respect, gave me the confidence that I was hovering over the target areas that I believe people could easily relate to and benefit from.

During my research, there was a specific story that intrigued, moved, and motivated me enough to continue down this path. It occurred while I was reading Viktor Frankl's *Man's Search for Meaning*. After being imprisoned in several of the worst Nazi concentration camps, Viktor Frankl was liberated in 1945. He dedicated the rest of his life to helping others find meaning in their lives. Among his many accomplishments, he delivered a series of collegiate lectures in locations over the world. It was during one of these lectures that Frankl was asked to express in one sentence what he thought the meaning of his own life was. He wrote the response on a piece of paper and asked his students to guess what he had written. One of the students correctly responded by stating, "The meaning of your life is to help others find the meaning of theirs."

This book was written for three reasons. The primary reason is to encourage you to contemplate and perhaps act on living a life with purpose, balancing physical, mental, emotional, and spiritual health, aging gracefully, and planning the kind of legacy to leave to loved ones and the world. It is designed to provide the general framework on how to live your best life with maximum impact.

The second reason is to generate a significant fundraising effort for multiple worthy charities, including but not limited to the Alzheimer's Association, National Breast Cancer Foundation, American Heart Association, National MS Society, and to other local charities. Admittedly, it is a lofty vision but it is a noble one. A significant portion of the profits received from the sale of this book will be donated to these charities. If you like this book, please consider buying it for friends and family who may benefit from the content. It is for good causes and thus becomes a win-win scenario.

Finally, the last reason is for me personally. The project has provided me with a renewed sense of purpose and meaning. It is part of my legacy. It has been a cathartic and enriching exercise. It has also satisfied an enormous urge I have to give back and help others.

Before we continue, here is a disclosure. I am not a trained dietician, nutritionist, personal trainer, estate planning attorney, doctor, psychiatrist, philosopher, clergyman, or other professional life coach. You may wonder that if I am not any of the aforementioned, then what authority do I have and why should you want to listen to me? Here is my response and my pitch. I have expertise and am well trained in behavioral finance along with the emotional impact that monetary and lifestyle decisions have on people and households. I am in the advice business and have been for decades, and although it is with an emphasis on monetary matters, part of my job is to ask probing personal questions and listen attentively. I hear and care about what people are interested in: their life stories, families, hobbies, goals, accomplishments, celebrations, health woes, and hardships. People are uniquely interesting and I love connecting with them on a business and personal level with genuine friendship, concern, compassion, and empathy. I do have professional credentials that provide authority regarding topics such as purpose and legacy planning. As for the rest of the topics, I have relied on the many other keen, qualified experts referenced throughout this book, supplemented by my own life experiences, observations, and insight.

This book is not technical or data driven. There are specific, straightforward recommendations—lots of them, in fact—along with general concepts and guidelines. It provides panoramic viewpoints of different perspectives, mindsets, and human behavior for how to live your best life. There are some sporadic humorous quotes mixed in to balance the tone to keep it light and entertaining. My writing style is rather straightforward and direct, and admittedly at times could be interpreted to some as being a little preachy. However, I believe and trust that you, the reader, can differentiate the finer areas where you could use some guidance and that you might appreciate the sincerity and bluntness of these points. Please understand that while there is an order and a flow to the material, many of the chapters and topics covered are connected and cross-referenced. There are overlapping messages and phrases, creating an intentional degree of redundancy. I feel that this repetition adds scope and depth and reinforces the underlying relevant points.

This book is divided into five parts. The first part dives into some valuable lessons and tips to motivate you to live your life with a sense of purpose and meaning. Having purpose is the spark that drives your energy and focus. It inspires and galvanizes your spirit and healthy life choices. All aspects of your life that are covered throughout this book feed off of having a clear path to follow. There are real-life examples of people you can learn from.

The second part includes the basics of how to maintain a healthy lifestyle. The content may seem too obvious, but it can be hard to accomplish on a daily basis. It is as much mental as it is physical. A variety of different areas are briefly covered. Each topic by itself may appear to be somewhat basic, but cumulatively and viewed under a wider lens, it becomes more constructive. Included are chapters on longevity research and aging.

The third part leaps into legacy planning, explaining what that entails and what people really want. It compares and contrasts traditional estate planning with legacy planning. Both are important aspects of legacy planning.

The fourth part contains fundamental insights about life that supplement the first three parts, with an emphasis on positive behavioral frames of mind.

The fifth part focuses on taking action. At the end of the day, it is about inspiring and encouraging you to think about making good life choices and then converting them into a realistic action plan.

Throughout this book are a few of my own original writings, which are meant to reinforce and augment the main points. The appendix showcases life lessons that I took away from working on this project.

Now here is a recommendation. As you are reading, select or highlight some of your favorite quotes or excerpts. You can also write them down in the notes section at the very end of this book, the ones that you connect with or that are positive affirmations of what you want to incorporate into your life. Repeat them to yourself on an ongoing basis. Assimilate them and have them become a part of your mindset and eventually a habit.

Another recommendation is to keep this book handy when you are having a bad day and need a pick-me-up. This is, in essence, a self-help book with realistic and positive messaging at its foundation. When necessary, reread the sections or chapters that are appropriate to get you back on track, boost your confidence, and realign your priorities.

Finally, this journey of researching for purpose, healthy lifestyle, and a notable legacy has led me down a path of self-actualization. It has reinforced the positive side of how to approach daily living with the realization of how much my life has been blessed. With some added perspective, appropriate lifestyle adjustments, and the right attitude, I truly hope that you will realize how much your life has been blessed too. At the end of each day, that's the best we can all strive for!

# PART 1

## Your Purpose
(Finding meaning in your life)

# CHAPTER 1

# Why Having Purpose Is Important

*Life without purpose is like a body without a soul.*
(Author Unknown)

Purpose is important because it drives other aspects of your life. Having a purpose or goals gives your life greater meaning and a sense of fulfillment. It provides an opportunity to deliver positive impact and social redeeming value to others or your community. It makes you feel that you can make a difference in the world, even in small ways.

It is also important to note that without purpose in your life, you may just be going through the motions aimlessly to get through each day, without really living or standing for something or someone. A suitable comparison would be like wandering randomly through a desert with nowhere to go and nothing of substance to do. Life is much more enriching and satisfying when you have purpose, meaning, and direction.

Bestselling author and spiritual leader Matthew Kelly elaborates further on having purpose:

*If there is purpose and meaning to our lives, then the highest levels of living must be linked to discovering that meaning and fulfilling that purpose. It stands to reason, then, that there should be a relationship between the purpose and meaning of life and our dreams.* (Kelly 1999)

He continues by adding:

*Energy is our most valuable resource, not time ... Energy is created by a sense of purpose and a lifestyle that integrates our legitimate needs, our deepest desires, and our talents.* (Kelly 1999)

We all have dreams. They can be manifestations of who we want to be and what we would like to accomplish. When we discover our potential, we find inner peace and true satisfaction. Through work and into retirement, you have the capability to not only survive but to thrive. When you have purpose, you also have renewable energy that feeds off of itself. You can see the world for its unlimited possibilities. You seek the solutions to many problems.

This then brings the distinction between purpose and mission. Your purpose is why you do something while your mission is what you do. When you have purpose, you have focus, which drives your passion. Life is challenging, yet more fun and interesting because finding purpose will influence your behavior, goals, motivation, lifestyle choices, and actions.

In his book *Tuesdays with Morrie,* author Mitch Albom interviews his former beloved college professor Morrie Schwartz to take a master one-on-one class about living and dying. One of Morrie's many pearls of wisdom is the following:

> *So many people walk around with a meaningless life. They seem half-asleep, even when they're busy doing things they think are important. This is because they're chasing the wrong things. The way you get meaning in your life is to devote yourself to loving others, devote yourself to the community around you, and devote yourself to creating something that gives you purpose and meaning.* (Albom 1997)

How do you search for and find purpose if you believe you have none? National Geographic Fellow and author Dan Buettner addresses this question in his book *The Blue Zones, Second Edition*. What he describes is simple, yet on target:

> *If you don't have a sense of purpose, how do you find it? Articulating your personal mission statement can be a good start. Begin by answering this question in a single, memorable sentence: Why do you get up in the morning? Consider what you're passionate about, how you enjoy using your talents, and what is truly important to you.* (Buettner 2012)

Age does not matter. You can find purpose and meaning at any age. It is never too late to start, just like it is never too late to form healthy habits in order to lead a healthier and balanced lifestyle. It is your desire, heart, mission, vision, passion, and even your love that matter. Don't be afraid to challenge yourself in your pursuit of finding purpose. In doing so, it leads to personal growth.

Purpose can evolve over time and should be revisited. It is personal and should come from within. It is possible to have multiple visions and multiple goals as long as there is room for more. There is no right or wrong way to find it but once you do, your daily lifestyle decisions will become pointed in that direction.

Here is a word of caution. There can sometimes be a fine line between being driven by purpose and being obsessed by it for too long. Balance is important as you want to stay fresh and not get burned out. It's okay to be consumed for a short period of time—say, to meet a deadline or when you are in a zone—but it can be counterproductive over extended periods.

It should be noted that there is a distinction between activity and purpose. An activity is something you either need or want to do. Examples of everyday activities that you need to do might be running errands, cleaning, working, or paying bills. Examples of activities you want to do might be taking a walk, watching television, reading a book, or going out to a restaurant or a show. Activities can fill up your days. Some may be important while others may be enjoyable, but they do not necessarily provide purpose. You come alive when you have purpose, something that motivates and drives you each day as a calling, not activities that just keep you busy.

In the chapters that follow, there will be role models and examples of what purpose can look like and mean, no matter what the circumstances are. While maintaining a healthy lifestyle is a key factor to leading a balanced life, you can still find purpose even if your health is compromised or you have experienced extreme suffering. Stay tuned!

# Purposeful Potpourri

*The two most important days in your life are the day you were born and the day you find out why.* (Mark Twain)

*The purpose of life, as far as I can tell ... is to find a mode of being that's so meaningful that the fact that life is suffering is no longer relevant.* (Jordan Peterson)

*The source of vision is inspiration. The source of inspiration is passion. The source of passion is purpose.* (Author Unknown)

*The greatest tragedy is not death but life without purpose.* (Rick Warren)

*The mystery of human existence lies not in just staying alive, but in finding something to live for.* (Fyodor Dostoyevsky)

*If you can tune into your purpose and really align with it, setting goals so that your vision is an expression of that purpose, then life flows much more easily.* (Jack Canfield)

*Life is meaningful when you are always looking to grow and working towards a goal.* (Les Brown)

*If you have a strong purpose in life, you don't have to be pushed. Your passion will drive you there.* (Roy T. Bennett)

# CHAPTER 2

# Viktor Frankl

*If there is meaning in life at all, then there must be meaning in suffering.* (Viktor Frankl)

Viktor Frankl was offered an immigration visa to escape Austria for the United States after Nazi Germany had occupied Austria and shortly before the United States entered into World War II in 1941. He hesitated as he grappled with the terrifying thought of having to leave his parents alone to then a still unknown but increasingly dangerous fate. Ultimately, he decided to turn down the visa after he saw a piece of marble lying on a table that his father had found on the site where the largest Viennese synagogue had been burned down by the National Socialists. It had originally been part of a tablet that the Ten Commandments had been inscribed on. There was one Hebrew letter engraved on it. When he asked his father which commandment it represented, his father answered, "Honor thy father and thy mother that thy days may be long upon the land."

When it comes to understanding purpose and the real meaning of life, Viktor Frankl was in a league of his own. He had so many wonderful life lessons from which we could all learn from. First, here is his background for those of you who have not heard about him before. This perspective is important to understand how much he suffered through, yet overcame, to rebuild his life and help countless others find purpose/meaning in their lives.

Viktor Frankl was born in 1905 and was a renowned Austrian-Jewish psychiatrist before Austria was annexed by Germany. He became a prisoner in four different Nazi prisoner-of-war concentration camps, including the "death camp" Auschwitz, from 1942 to 1945. Each day was a struggle to just stay alive. Prisoners were treated as subhuman; lives were debased and devalued. Death, malnutrition, and disease were pervasive everywhere and every day. While Frankl somehow survived, his parents, brother, and pregnant wife were murdered in the Holocaust in these same camps.

Viktor Frankl was liberated by the Allies near the end of the war, which is when he learned about the fate of his loved ones. He dedicated the rest of his life to helping others cope with suffering and to find meaning in their lives. He invented and developed logotherapy, which is the discovery and pursuit of helping people find meaning and purpose in their own lives. Frankl was an MD and earned his PhD after the war in 1948. While he returned to Austria and remarried, he was also a visiting professor and lecturer at many locations, including Harvard and Stanford. He published over thirty books, the most famous being *Man's Search for Meaning*, which is still considered one of the most influential books of all time. Viktor Frankl passed away in 1997.

In one of his other books, *Yes to Life*, Viktor Frankl summarizes what it was like living in the Nazi concentration camps on a daily basis:

*What remained was the individual person, the human being—and nothing else. Everything had fallen away from him during those years; money, power, fame; nothing was certain for him anymore: not life, not health, not happiness: all that had been called into question for him: vanity, ambition, relationships. Everything was reduced to bare existence.* (Frankl 2020)

He went on to state that self-preservation was his only goal each and every day, while so many around him lost hope and gave up on life. Frankl never gave up hope and kept his dreams of seeing his wife and continuing his work after the war. That hope provided him the drive to survive and gave him purpose to live. He also acknowledged that there was an element of luck to his survival since on the day he arrived at Auschwitz, a guard briefly looked him over and waved him over to one side. Unbeknownst to him at the time, this spontaneous decision meant he was selected to work and live for another day. The prisoners sent to the other side, which he speculated was around 90 percent, were sent to their deaths within hours.

In the foreword to a more updated version of *Man's Search for Meaning*, esteemed rabbi and author Harold Kushner wrote this:

*Frankl's most enduring insight, one that I have called on often in my own life and in countless counseling situations: Forces beyond your control can take away everything you possess except one thing, your freedom to choose how you will respond to the situation. You cannot control what*

*happens in your life, but you can always control what you will feel and do about what happens to you.*
(Frankl 2006 edition)

What is remarkable about Frankl's life is that he rejected the idea of collective guilt and revenge for his suffering and losses. He did not ask for apologies or reparations from the Germans or even fellow Austrians who participated in the Nazi atrocities. Instead he focused his life work on the healing of a person's soul. He believed that if one exists in this world at all, then each one makes the world and the life in it meaningful. Therefore, human life never ceases to have meaning, and that striving to find a meaning in one's life is or should be the primary driving force in man.

According to the principles of logotherapy (which still exists today) there are three different ways you can find meaning in life. Here is Viktor Frankl again in his own words:

*As logotherapy teaches, there are three main avenues which one arrives at meaning in life. The first is by creating a work or doing a deed. The second is by experiencing something or encountering someone; in other words, meaning can be found not only in work but also in love ... Most important, however, is the third avenue to meaning in life; even the hopeless victim of a hopeless situation, facing a fate he cannot change, may rise above himself, may grow beyond himself, and by doing so change himself.*
(Frankl 2006 edition)

Let us dig a little deeper into each of these three ways. The first is the easiest to understand. The act of creating, inventing, or collaborating for something of significance can bring purpose and meaning. It is about making a difference in the world. The second is to do something out of love like caring for someone other than yourself or by giving yourself to a cause to serve. The third is through unavoidable suffering (like Frankl suffered) and by finding the meaning and acting upon it in a positive way. Suffering itself has no meaning; it is more about the way you respond to it. Suffering ceases to be suffering at the moment that meaning is found. However, despair is suffering without meaning. He elaborates further by adding that personal choices, activities, relationships, hobbies, and even simple pleasures can provide meaning.

What does it take to endure the suffering that someone like Viktor Frankl had to endure? The answer is the attitude toward life challenges and opportunities. A positive attitude brings hope and helps enable a person to endure suffering. It provides the courage to continue and not give up. A negative attitude intensifies the pain and deepens the disappointments. Over time, the negativity could diminish any semblance of happiness and lead to depression. An ongoing disposition of gloom could then overwhelm any potential feelings of hope.

When a person has a consistent doom and gloom attitude, he or she may not only be more prone to depression but also potential thoughts of suicide. Frankl believed that in all these dark moments, there was a solution to the problem, a meaning to their life. However, that person must live to see the day the change happens. Therefore, survival is critical. The same holds true for addictions such as drugs, alcohol abuse, or gambling, in which there is often a sense of not belonging or that life has no meaning.

If you think of yourself as a victim, then that line of thinking stays with you in your subconscious mind. The more you think about it, the more your hate grows. Your negative emotions then crowd out your ability to experience joy, happiness, freedom, and peace of mind. It permeates down to your very soul.

The first half of *Man's Search for Meaning* is Viktor Frankl's account of his years as a war prisoner, with an emphasis on the first day, what everyday life was like, and on the day he was liberated. That part of the book was written in 1945 while his thoughts and memories were still fresh. His goal was to prove that life held potential meaning even under the most cruel and miserable conditions. It was in the camps that he tried to inspire others and give them the will to live. Here is an excerpt of the message he conveyed to his fellow prisoners:

> *... I spoke of the many opportunities of giving life a meaning. I told my comrades ... that human life, under any circumstances, never ceases to have a meaning, and that this infinite meaning of life includes suffering and dying, privation and death ... They must not lose hope but should keep their courage in the certainty that the hopelessness of our struggle did not detract from its dignity and its meaning.* (Frankl 2006 edition)

Purpose is something that is discovered and varies from person to person. It is found in the context of our lives. It is not about keeping score of our successes but rather through our contributions, relationships, experiences, and attitudes. The world learned a lot from the lessons that Viktor Frankl taught us. It is our responsibility to share his wisdom, apply it, and pass it on from generation to generation to ensure that his lessons are never forgotten.

# Meaningful Minds

*Our greatest freedom is the freedom to choose our attitude.* (Viktor Frankl)

(NOTE: This next quote is exceptional because it advances the case to sometimes take a few extra moments to carefully think and substitute an emotional or spontaneous response with more of an astute and deliberate one).

*Between stimulus and response there is a space. In that space is our power to choose our response. In our response lies our growth and our freedom.* (Viktor Frankl)

*When a man cannot find meaning, he numbs himself with pleasure.* (Viktor Frankl)

*For the meaning of life differs from man to man, from day to day, and from hour to hour. What matters, therefore, is not the meaning of life in general but rather the specific meaning of a person's life at a given moment.* (Viktor Frankl)

*Suffering has been stronger than all other teaching and has taught me to understand what your heart used to be. I have been bent and broken, but—I hope—into a better shape.* (Charles Dickens)

*Out of suffering have emerged the strongest souls; the most massive characters are seared with scars.* (Khalil Gibran)

*He who has a why to live can bear almost any how.*
(Friedrich Nietzsche)

*To live is to suffer, to survive is to find some meaning in the suffering.*
(Friedrich Nietzsche)

*That which does not kill us makes us stronger.*
(Friedrich Nietzsche)

# CHAPTER 3

# Nelson Mandela

*It is in your hands to create a better world for all who live in it.*
(Nelson Mandela)

N elson Mandela lived a life with purpose and left a legendary legacy. He survived through a long-suffering ordeal of being falsely imprisoned for twenty-seven years. His prison cell was small, he used a bucket for a toilet, he slept on the floor, and he performed hard labor. Communication to the outside world was extremely limited, and thus he had much time to think, evolve, and grow from within. While in prison his reputation continued to grow as well as his mission of equality. With maturity over time, he found the strength and courage to forgive his oppressors. He never gave up hope in his lifelong struggle to end South Africa's apartheid system of true racism, division, and discrimination. He became a champion of unification and peace as well as a shining symbol of grace and dignity.

He kept true to his moral principles at all times. In 1964 while on trial and facing a possible death sentence, here were his now-immortalized words to the court:

*I have fought against white domination, and I have fought against black domination. I have cherished the ideal of a democratic and free society in which all persons live together in harmony and with equal opportunities. It is an ideal which I hope to live for and to achieve. But if needs be, it is an ideal for which I am prepared to die.*
(Nelson Mandela Centre of Memory-Biography)

Mandela received the Nobel Peace Prize in 1993 and was elected president of South Africa in 1994, then served in that capacity for five years. He continued to work through efforts such as the Nelson Mandela Children's Fund and the Nelson Mandela Foundation. He was an international figure and supported a variety of social and human rights organizations.

How was he able to transcend his hatred to become a peacemaker and provide such extraordinary leadership to his country? How was he able to resist the temptation for revenge during all those years while having to endure life as a political prisoner in a small prison cell? How was he able to move on despite the fact he was not able to watch his children grow up while losing his marriage and the best years of his life?

His answer was that if he continued to hate them, then he would still be their prisoner. He wanted to be free, so he was able to let go of his hate. Mandela was once asked in those long years on Robben Island and elsewhere if there was something that helped sustain his spirits and gave him the strength to sustain his will to survive. He replied that he regularly recited the poem "Invictus," written by William Ernest Henley in 1875. The word invictus means unconquerable. It is a powerful poem with an inspirational message. Here it is. Read it carefully as the underlying theme can apply to anyone having endured periods of adversity or challenging times.

# Invictus

*Out of the night that covers me,*
*Black as the Pit from pole to pole,*
*I thank whatever gods may be*
*For my unconquerable soul.*
*In the fell clutch of circumstance*
*I have not winced nor cried aloud.*
*Under the bludgeonings of chance*
*My head is bloody, but unbowed.*
*Beyond this place of wrath and tears*
*Looms but the horror of the shade,*
*And yet the menace of the years*
*Finds, and shall find me, unafraid.*
*It matters not how strait the gate,*
*How charged with punishments the scroll,*
*I am the master of my fate:*
*I am the captain of my soul.*

There are many life lessons to be learned from Nelson Mandela's heroism and sacrifices that can be applied to our everyday lives. In researching the life of Nelson Mandela, I discovered lessons that reflect some of the common points of this book:

- Have core principles that define who you are and what you stand for.
- Never lose hope even against all odds.
- Stand firm with your convictions and stay true to yourself.
- Learn to lose the hatred and the demons living inside of you.
- Take control of your emotions and your attitude.
- Stay patient; maintain self-control in spite of any setbacks.
- Don't be overcome by seemingly overwhelming challenges.
- Evolve and never be afraid to learn and grow as a person.
- Take the time to know yourself better, particularly your mind and your feelings.
- Overcome the bad within you and develop the good inside you.
- Meditate, when needed, to calm your emotions.
- Find something that gives you inner strength and inspiration to persevere during times of extreme hardships.
- Never give up on yourself or on life.
- Learn to forgive others and move on.
- Be a leader and unify through inspiration, not demonization.
- Be kind and generous with your time and money (as through charities).
- Be a positive role model and a force for good in the world.

Nelson Mandela had passion in his soul that drove him. His core values gave him a foundation, and his passion brought him a purpose in life. By staying the course even through suffering, he displayed extraordinary patience and exemplary leadership skills. A sense of purpose led to positive impact and global contributions. It was his actions and demeanor that made him a change agent and a legend. Ultimately, through his accomplishments, his legacy was formed and cast in stone. His life influenced the soul of a nation as well as the world. It was a meaningful life!

## Great Mandela Quotes

*It always seems impossible until it's done.* (Nelson Mandela)

*There can be no greater gift than that of giving one's time and energy to help others without expecting anything in return.* (Nelson Mandela)

*If you want to make peace with your enemy, you have to work with your enemy. Then he becomes your partner.* (Nelson Mandela)

*Courageous people do not fear forgiving, for the sake of peace.* (Nelson Mandela)

*Everyone can rise above their circumstances and achieve success if they are dedicated to and passionate about what they do.* (Nelson Mandela)

*There were many dark moments when my faith in humanity was sorely tested, but I would not and could not give myself up to despair. That way lays defeat and death.* (Nelson Mandela)

## CHAPTER 4

# Charles Krauthammer

*You're betraying your whole life if you don't say what you think and you don't say it honestly and bluntly.* (Charles Krauthammer)

C harles Krauthammer was a positive role model for many people, including myself. He was able to overcome a personal tragedy to subsequently find his purpose in life and leave an indelible legacy. He was a Pulitzer Prize-winning syndicated columnist and political commentator. What sets him apart from others was not only his brilliant analytical mind and his remarkable ability to analyze news with such detail and clarity, but also his capacity to shape his life and control his destiny despite having a serious physical handicap.

He was at the end of his freshman year at medical school in 1972 when he had a diving accident at age twenty-two, which severed his cervical spinal cord and left him permanently paralyzed from the waist down. After some recovery time, he finished medical school with the help of some caring professors. He completed a residency in psychiatry and afterward became board certified. What is impressive is that he finished his freshman year while still in traction. Professors showed up at his bedside and presented him the lectures while projecting the slides on the ceiling. Charles was determined to be the best he could be despite the circumstances. Some years later he reinvented himself again. He changed direction in his professional life and moved on to his ultimate career path as a columnist and political pundit.

What was so impressive about Krauthammer was that he never let his disability get in the way of his accomplishments in work or in life. He never complained or let the story be about himself. His gifted communication skills and dry wit were notable, and he was never condescending when he wrote his columns or spoke about issues. He had an amazing attitude, and he never gave up on life even when his outlook looked grim after his accident. In his professional life, while his political affiliation evolved over time, he always stayed true to the core principles he believed in. He was humble and down to earth. His civility, astute critiques, and integrity were distinguishable, clear, and noticeable. As a result, his fan base was enormous and he was admired and respected by so many people. He was never looking to impress anyone but simply spoke and wrote with conviction.

Some of his articles were thought-provoking. For example, here is an excerpt from an article he wrote in 1999:

> *It is just a parlor game, but since it only plays once every hundred years, it is hard to resist. Person of the century? Time magazine offered Albert Einstein, an interesting and solid choice. Unfortunately, it is wrong. The only possible answer is Winston Churchill. Why? Because Churchill carries that absolutely required criterion: indispensability.*

*Without Winston Churchill the world today would be unrecognizable—dark, impoverished, tortured . . . every once in a while, a single person arises without whom everything would be different. Such a man was Churchill.* (Krauthammer 2013)

Now use your imagination. Do you agree with Charles? Who would you have voted for as "person of the century"? As an aside, if you had the opportunity, who would you like to spend an evening with regardless of the era they lived in? (On a personal level, I might have selected Charles himself.)

Now fast-forward to the present. Who is your role model in life? Who can you reach out to who can help you when you need it the most? Who can you lean on for advice or to function as a sounding board to aid you on your path to finding or maintaining your purpose?

People like Viktor Frankl, Nelson Mandela, and Charles Krauthammer overcame adversity in their lives. They were able to reset their lives without asking for pity or holding grudges. They found meaning and purpose in their lives and left powerful legacies. You don't need to overcome the suffering and adversity they experienced to find purpose, but hopefully you can find some inspiration from their diverse backgrounds and life stories to find purpose in your life.

Charles Krauthammer died in 2018 from intestinal cancer. His last published words to his many fans were moving and speak of the character, grace, and dignity he had until the very end of his life:

*I have been uncharacteristically silent these past ten months. I had thought that silence would soon be coming to an end, but I'm afraid I must tell you now that fate has decided on a different course for me. In August of last year, I underwent surgery to remove a cancerous tumor in my abdomen. That operation was thought to have been a success, but it caused a cascade of secondary complications—which I have been fighting in hospital ever since. It was a long and hard fight with many setbacks, but I was steadily, if slowly, overcoming each obstacle along the way and gradually making my way back to health. However, recent tests have revealed that the cancer has returned . . . My doctors tell me that their best estimate is that I have only a few weeks to live. This is my final verdict. My fight is over . . . Lastly, I thank my colleagues, my readers and my viewers, who made my career possible and given consequence to my life's work. I believe that the pursuit of truth and right ideas through honest debate and rigorous argument is a noble undertaking. I am grateful to have played a small role in the conversations that have helped guide this extraordinary nation's destiny. I leave this life with no regrets. It was a wonderful life—full and complete with the great loves and great endeavors that make it worth living. I am sad to leave, but I leave with the knowledge that I lived the life that I intended.* (Krauthammer 2018)

Simply stated, the world is a better place because Charles Krauthammer lived in it, as he was a shining beacon of honesty, morality, and wisdom. His life was a perfect textbook of how to overcome extreme obstacles, yet lead a balanced, disciplined, and full life of distinction. His physical handicap did not stop him or dampen his spirits for long as he was able to forge ahead with his life, goals, vision, and ambitions. He had purpose in his life and left a lasting legacy. Have perspective as you reflect on your life, your issues, and your dreams. Learn from his life story as you focus on your own path forward.

## Common Sense from Charles

*Fight for what you know to be right. Don't give up.*
(Charles Krauthammer)

*It is fate, destiny, nemesis. Perhaps the dawning of knowledge, the coming of sin. Or more prosaically, the catastrophe that awaits everyone from a single false move, wrong turn, fatal encounter. Every life has such a moment. What distinguishes us is whether— and how—we ever come back.* (Charles Krauthammer)

*Better to be paralyzed from the neck down than the neck up.*
(Charles Krauthammer)

# CHAPTER 5

# Faith and Religion

*All religions must be tolerated . . . for every man must*
*get to heaven in his own way.* (Epictetus)

I am approaching this chapter from a macro-overview and spiritual level, not from a biblical or deeply religious standpoint. My objective is to point out how faith and religion can provide the confidence you need as well as the impetus to focus on your purpose in life and to stay on the right track. Faith and religion can provide the backbone and inner strength you need to live a life of integrity and meaning. Since people are of diverse backgrounds, my hope is that this theme can be universally applied to everyone who believes in the goodness of what faith and religion bring to their lives, regardless of whether they belong to a church, synagogue, mosque, or anything else. It applies to anyone who believes in God, the son of God, any higher authority, or other form of deities. Although atheists do not believe in God, they have their own alternative belief system, which provides them a form of strength and tranquility. It is my opinion that although you do not need to be religious to have purpose or faith, that faith is often augmented for those with core religious values and convictions.

Faith can be applied in a religious or non-religious setting. The definition of faith literally is the belief in anything as a code of conduct, loyalty to a person, or a belief system such as a religious doctrine. It is having confidence in a person or thing. At its essence, faith emits hope and trust in the greater good or in the belief of God. The expressions "leap of faith" or "blind faith" are used when someone trusts that there will be a positive outcome even without definitive proof.

Human beings are social beings, and we generally have a need to be accepted and liked. We have a sense of needing to belong and are interdependent with each other for support and socialization. We are influenced by friends, family, and peers. We generally tend to be spiritual, which often gives us direction and clarity. It also brings wants and desires. Distinguishing between the two can lead to purpose and meaning. Matthew Kelly explains it this way:

> *We must learn to move beyond our superficial wants and begin to discover our deepest desires. The difference between our wants and our deepest desires is meaning. A desire is a want with meaning… The shallow desire has only one thing in mind, the instant gratification of pleasure. Our spiritual wants are not even able to take into consideration the future pain that a present pleasure can cause us.* (Kelly 1999)

He goes on to say that when you are able to intersect your deepest desires (your passion) with your legitimate needs (what you need to thrive) and your unique talents (what you are born to do), then you come away with the best version of yourself. In that regard, you are better equipped to find your purpose.

Now let's pivot and talk more about the role of religion. In my opinion, it helps you toe the line and differentiate between right from wrong, or good and evil. It provides the moral compass you need to resist temptation and the resiliency to not be destroyed by life's unfairness. It is there to help guide you and provide the resources to live a meaningful life. You can then find the courage to go on even when you believe that life is unfair. There is both power and comfort in having strong religious convictions, in daily prayer, and in faith in eternal life. Religion has been the vehicle for turning many people's lives around, those who were suffering, self-destructing, or heading down the wrong path.

No discussion about faith and religion and how it brings purpose would be remotely complete without bringing up the importance of God. Harold Kushner elaborates on the role of God in this way:

> *God's role is not to make our lives easier, to make the hard things go away, or to do them for us. God's role is to give us the vision to know what we need to do, to bless us with the qualities of soul that we will need in order to do them ourselves, no matter how hard they may be, and to accompany us on that journey. (Kushner 2015)*

He continues by discussing problems, illness, accidents, and anguish:

*God does not send the problem; genetics, chance, and bad luck do that. And God cannot make the problem go away, no matter how many prayers and good deeds we offer. What God does is promise us, I will be with you; you will feel burdened, but you will never feel abandoned.* (Kushner 2015)

Harold Kushner claims that God is the small voice that gives you faith and courage when you need it the most. While we normally use our left brain for facts and logic, we use our right brain to tell a story or for intuition and feelings. God lives in the right brain: in our visualizations, emotions, and convictions.

When it comes to religious views, we should be accepting of others. If it works for you, why should we deprive you of your convictions and beliefs? How can anyone judge someone else and know for certain who is right and who is wrong? Religious choices and religious freedom are sacrosanct and should be left to the discretion of each individual to decide what works for him or her.

What is the difference between spirituality, theology, religion, and faith? How does that lead to purpose? Spirituality is what you feel, theology is what you believe, religion is what you do, and faith is the complete trust you have in someone or something. Having faith is about cultivating a positive spirit. It's about being optimistic that you will fulfill your goals, your dreams, and your hopes. It is also about helping others when they need an emotional uplift. Helping others can give you purpose in life. Sometimes the best way for you to feel better about yourself is to comfort those who need aid.

Daniel Cohen describes finding faith this way:

*The principle of finding faith offers a path to transforming our heightened consciousness in a moment of crisis to a sustainable awareness of the opportunities and blessings of every day.* (Cohen 2017)

Faith helps you be better equipped to cope with whatever life throws your way. As you know, life is a journey with many obstacles coming at us from different directions. Having spiritual and mental fortitude is a healthy positive mechanism to help us cope and adapt.

One of the primary functions of religion is to bring people together as a community, increasing friendship and common values. That increases joy and reduces sorrow. It is also there to lift you up when you need it the most.

Religion at its best can solidify your purpose and help you overcome hardships. However, be aware that religion can also be used as a shield to hide immoral, unethical, illegal, or criminal acts. Always be mindful of one's true intentions. There have been many crimes or immoral acts committed throughout history in the name of religion. Never lose your ability to slow down and use your left brain when things just do not seem right.

If you ever do find yourself in trouble, at a point where life is dragging you down, where you have lost your sense of purpose, or are at times being dominated by the demons in your head, perhaps you may then want to consider reaching out and staying closer to God to guide and lead you back out of harm's way to help restore your faith and sense of purpose.

Finding your purpose through faith, religion, or other forms of enlightenment will differ based upon your belief system and spirituality. In searching for purpose, figure out what makes your soul come alive with passion. The journey of your soul is complicated because life is complicated and sometimes turbulent. Having faith is a great step in the right direction as it evokes a positive attitude, which is the subject of the next chapter.

# Faithful Findings

*Love the Lord your God with all your heart and with all your soul and with all your mind.* (Jesus Christ)

*Prayer is not asking. It is a longing of the soul. It is daily admission of one's weakness. It is better in prayer to have a heart without words than words without a heart.* (Mahatma Gandhi)

*None can believe how powerful prayer is, and what it is able to effect, but those who have learned it by experience.* (Martin Luther)

*The greatest of wealth is the richness of the soul.* (Muhammad)

*Prayer is not asking. Prayer is putting oneself in the hands of God, at his disposition, and listening to his voice in the depth of our hearts.* (Mother Teresa)

*To one who has faith, no explanation is necessary. To one without faith, no explanation is possible.* (Thomas Aquinas)

*All the commandments: You shall not commit adultery, you shall not kill, you shall not steal, you shall not covet, and so on, are summed up in this single command: You must love your neighbor as yourself.* (Jesus Christ)

*There are two primary forces in this world, fear and faith. Fear can move you to destructiveness or sickness or failure. Only in rare instances will it motivate you to accomplishment. But faith is a greater force. Faith can drive itself into your consciousness and set you free from fear forever.* (Norman Vincent Peale)

*Be not forgetful of prayer. Every time you pray, if your prayer is sincere, there will be new feeling and new meaning in it, which will give you fresh courage, and you will understand that prayer is an education.* (Fyodor Dostoevsky)

# CHAPTER 6

# Attitude

*Very little is needed to make a happy life; it is all within yourself,*
*in your way of thinking.* (Marcus Aurelius)

World-renowned physicist Stephen Hawking was diagnosed at age twenty-one with early-onset and slow-progressing ALS disease that eventually paralyzed him and his ability to talk. However, he did not let the disease impact his drive and determination, which allowed him to have a prestigious, accomplished, and meaningful life.

Attitude is everything. It sets the tone and impacts you and those around you. The importance of having a good attitude can never be overstated as the quality of your attitude will most likely have a direct correlation to your happiness or misery levels. It will impact your success in life and your ability to accomplish tasks or goals through both easy and difficult times. I believe that in order to excel at work and in life, two of the most important attributes are attitude and effort, at times even more than experience. Someone without the right background but who is motivated enough to learn, work hard, and possess a great attitude is worth more to an employer than someone with more experience but has a poor work ethic, does not work hard, or is high maintenance. Of course, education and experience are important. For example, a surgeon needs both education and experience to operate or perform surgery. However, once those requirements are attained, then attitude and effort become an occupational factor for determining ongoing success.

There is a difference, though, between someone with a positive attitude and someone who has a positive attitude all the time. We are all human and it is just not realistic to be overly optimistic all the time. You cannot be expected to be positive when things are going the wrong way or are too stressful since it could lead to improper decisions being made. However, you can be calm and somewhat neutral in your approach in those situations. Learn to take a few deep breaths and then think through the best course of action. Being able to work through these moments and feelings will help you in indeterminable ways.

A suitable and successful attitude will help you with achieving your goals and improving your productivity. It will crowd out the negativity in your life and will make you more likable and someone whom others want to be with. It will also help you in finding, maintaining, and celebrating everything: your goals, purpose, and legacy.

When it comes to achieving a healthy lifestyle, managing stress and having the proper mindset are important to staying vibrant, healthy, and young at heart. Life is about having proper balance, and choosing the right and best attitude at the right times will help you get farther. You will be able to better manage constructive criticism without taking it personally. The enjoyment that you get from seemingly simple daily functions or tasks will come to you naturally. Being able to laugh more about life's little moments sure seems more fun than complaining about everything that you dislike.

When you are upset about something that breaks or something that goes wrong that is beyond your control such as a home or car issue, consider framing the issue a different way. Instead of complaining about what went wrong, try focusing on what went right. If someone makes an unintentional mistake that sets you back, consider how fortunate you are that you are able to find the mistake, correct it, and be able to move on with some minor but temporary inconvenience. You should realize that these are minor hiccups in the scope of the grand issues of the universe. Perspective matters. Focus on what really matters.

Viktor Frankl had it right, and I'll repeat this quote for the second time in this book: "Our greatest freedom is the freedom to choose our attitude." It is so profound and true. You cannot control what happens to you during the course of a day, but you can control how you react. When you are able to manage your emotions, then you are the master of your destiny, no matter how dire the circumstances are.

- Keep your attitude in check, as it impacts everything you do and feel.
- You have the freedom to control your attitude. It is within your power.
- Stay true to yourself, your convictions, your values, and your faith.
- Do not forget to keep your head up, be yourself, stay calm, and breathe.
- You always get a second chance; it's called tomorrow.

# Attitude Affirmations

*If you don't like something, change it. If you can't change it, change your attitude.* (Maya Angelou)

*Our attitudes toward life determine life's attitude toward us.* (Earl Nightingale)

*Each day is a gift—a new beginning—bound out of bed with the enthusiasm of a child.* (Joyce Moon)

*Every now and then go away, have a little relaxation, for when you come back to work your judgment will be surer. Go some distance away because the work appears smaller and more of it can be taken in at a glance and a lack of harmony and proportion is more readily seen.* (Leonardo Da Vinci)

*Nothing can stop the man with the right mental attitude from achieving his goal; nothing on earth can help the man with the wrong mental attitude.* (Thomas Jefferson)

*Human beings by changing the inner attitudes of their minds can change the outer aspects of their lives.* (William James)

*Our attitudes control our lives. Attitudes are a secret power working twenty-four hours a day, for good or bad. It is of paramount importance that we know how to harness and control this great force.* (Irving Berlin)

*You cannot control what happens to you, but you can control your attitude toward what happens to you, and in that, you will be mastering change rather than allowing it to master you.* (Brian Tracy)

*Whenever you're in conflict with someone, there is one factor that can make the difference between damaging your relationship and deepening it. That factor is attitude.* (William James)

*Don't go around saying the world owes you a living. The world owes you nothing. It was here first.* (Mark Twain)

## CHAPTER 7

# Never Give Up

*Our greatest weakness lies in giving up. The most certain way to succeed is always to try just one more time.* (Thomas Edison)

Michael Jordan is a great example of never giving up. As a sophomore in high school, he was cut from his varsity basketball team. This just fueled his desire to learn from this and improve his overall game. You already know the rest of the story. He ultimately became one of the greatest basketball players of all time.

At different points in life, you will fail at something. It is inevitable. Nothing ever goes completely according to plan. We will run into a seemingly difficult or impossible obstacle. It feels like hitting a brick wall. In those times, we need to display resolve, grit, and determination. While never giving up can apply to all aspects of your life, we'll keep our focus on how it applies to purpose.

If you find your passion but come across a difficult situation, you can either engage the matter openly, change your attitude, or change the environment. However, don't give up on anything that gives you excitement or meaning. Never give up on yourself because you have infinite potential for anything.

If failure is imminent, learn from it. Embrace failure (after the initial emotions wear down) for what it is. Take responsibility for your share and do not blame others. For that matter, be wary of taking all the credit for any successes. Be humble and give credit to others when it's due.

Bumps in the road may appear to get in the way of your goals and dreams. That's just part of life. The key is how you adjust accordingly. Learn to be mentally tough and not easily rattled. Do not let adversarial people or contentious conditions live in your head. Think of solutions or ways around the problems and keep moving forward.

One of the most inspirational and brilliant speeches on this topic ever made was by Winston Churchill, made as prime minister during World War II. At the time this speech was delivered, October 29, 1941, the situation in Great Britain was tense and quite uncertain. It was between the Battle of Britain (the fierce air battle between Great Britain and Nazi Germany from July 1940 to May 1941) and the time the United States entered the war on December 7, 1941 (the day of infamy, after the attack on Pearl Harbor). Churchill's leadership and convictions helped unify a worried nation at a time when the nation needed it the most. Here is the most famous excerpt of that speech:

> *Never give in, never give in. Never, never, never, never— in nothing, great or small, large, or petty—never give in, except to convictions of honor and good sense. Never yield to force. Never yield to the apparently overwhelming might of the enemy.*

Remember that you can find meaning in failure, just like you can from suffering. Entrepreneurs fail. Innovators fail. In baseball, batters are All-Stars despite failing to get a hit roughly 70 percent of the time. Learn from failure as it can make you stronger. Never give up on your dreams. Believe in yourself. Do not back down even if you are a little frightened. The only way you can truly fail is when you give up. Be courageous, confront your fears, and keep your passions alive.

If you have a bad moment, a bad day, or a bad week, then stop and reflect. Revisit the situation, take your emotions out of the equation, and analyze what happened. Is there anything you would or should have done differently? What did you learn? Are there action steps that you can take? If so, what do you need to do? Are there any resources available or people that you can lean on and rely on for advice or support? Failure can be a gift, and if you've learned from it, then it's really not a failure.

It is your life and your future direction that you are shaping. Be both an optimist and a realist in your work ethic. Stay with your passions and continue to search for meaning and purpose. Whatever you are feeling mentally, physically, emotionally, or spiritually, today is a new day. If today doesn't work out, there is always tomorrow. Just hang in there. Stay positive, work hard, make it happen, and never give up!

# Never Give Up Nuggets

*Failure is success if we learn from it.* (Malcolm Forbes)

*However difficult life may seem, there is always something you can do and succeed at. It matters that you don't just give up.* (Stephen Hawking)

*Never give up on a dream just because of the time it will take to accomplish it. The time will pass anyway.* (Earl Nightingale)

*Stay strong, stay positive, and never give up.* (Roy T. Bennett)

*A life spent making mistakes is not only more honorable, but more useful than a life spent doing nothing.* (George Bernard Shaw)

*It is impossible to live without failing at something unless you have lived so cautiously that you might as well not lived at all, in which case you have failed by default.* (J. K. Rowling)

*Failure is a bend in the road, not the end of the road. Learn from failure and keep moving forward.* (Roy T. Bennett)

*I have not failed. I just found 10,000 ways that won't work.* (Thomas Edison)

*The man who never makes a mistake must get tired of doing nothing.* (Will Rogers)

*When you think about quitting, think about why you started.*
(Author Unknown)

*Our greatest glory is not in never falling but in rising every time
we fall.* (Confucius)

(NOTE: The quote below is one of my favorite quotes. I hope you
will take extra time to ponder it.)

*Nothing in the world can take the place of persistence. Talent
will not; nothing is more common than unsuccessful men with
talent. Genius will not; unrewarded genius is almost a proverb.
Education will not; the world is full of educated derelicts.
Persistence and determination alone are omnipotent.*
(Calvin Coolidge)

## CHAPTER 8

# Find Your Path

*The purpose of life is a life with purpose.* (Robert Byrne)

Before Walt Disney built his empire, he had to find his path to success. When he was young, he was criticized by his newspaper editor, who thought he had no talent as an illustrator. This motivated and helped him overcome his fears of failure and ultimately provided the impetus for him to discover his true purpose and become the visionary and entrepreneur that he was.

When you have a purpose in life, there is an intangible motivating element that drives you each day and gives you direction: something that energizes and makes your spirit come alive. You are able to answer the question as to why you get up in the morning. I am not suggesting everyone needs a purpose to enjoy and appreciate life and all the benefits that come with it. I am suggesting that you find meaning and purpose in whatever path you follow to find your life enriched and fulfilled. There is no particular right or wrong path for seeking gratification and contentment. That is for each of you to figure out. The bigger point is that if you have not found your path, but you would like to, it is never too late. Maintain a positive attitude, contemplate your goals, get organized, have a realistic action plan, implement it, reassess it periodically, stay with it, and never give up.

Dr. Mark Shrime, a surgeon and author, has the following opinion about going forward:

> *Purpose, meaning, and contentment exist when why is at the center, and when we construct our paths to lead to it. Not the other way around.* (Shrime 2022)

While leading a healthy life makes it easier to stay focused on seeking and finding purpose and meaning in life, it is not necessarily a prerequisite for finding your purpose. As you saw in the three examples of Viktor Frankl, Nelson Mandela, and Charles Krauthammer, there are other ways to find meaning such as through unavoidable suffering. Since no one typically volunteers to go that route, you can find your purpose in other ways.

Having a purpose can evolve with age, maturity, education, and experience. It can change due to marriage, families, career paths, or as life dictates. Sometimes you are too wrapped up in everyday matters to find meaning and sometimes it is staring you in the face and you do not see it. As you age and approach your life expectancy, finding purpose typically becomes more time-sensitive, relevant, and a higher priority.

When you have a purpose, it is easier to seize the day. When you find purpose and meaning in your life, you can see the world for its possibilities, not its issues. (Purpose and meaning are used interchangeably throughout the book but they both really mean the exact same thing.) Having a purpose gives you a reason to stay focused, be organized, lead a balanced life, and discover your renewable energy. Having a purpose keeps you young at heart. It allows you to discover or rediscover your potential. Even when you are retired, you are not retired from life. Take advantage of the time you have to find meaning. When you find it, life is more gratifying.

Everyone has some specialized talent or abilities. Seek to discover what your unique interests are and match those with your talents. Never stop learning along the way. Commit yourself to being the best you can be. When you fail, keep your head up, pick yourself off the ground, refocus, and try it again. Through hard times, smile, stay strong, have the courage to continue, persevere, and even laugh.

Having purpose builds character. It brings self-discipline and personal growth. It brings success and fulfillment as you continue to evolve and develop into the life you choose to live. When you accomplish something successfully, you will feel proud and content because:

- you have made a difference in something or for someone.
- you have done something good in your community or in the world.
- you have accomplished a goal that brings with it a sense of satisfaction and confidence.

Matthew Kelly had an excellent observation when he said:

*What we do in the span of our lives may bring us financial rewards, status, fame, power, and unimaginable possessions, but lasting happiness and fulfillment are not the by-products of doing and having ... The meaning and purpose of life is for you to become the-best-version-of-yourself.* (Kelly 1999)

Desire, ambition, and passion are wonderful galvanizing forces. When you have them, you can embrace who you are. You are calmer and relaxed because you have longer-term guidance. Even when things do not go exactly as planned, you are motivated enough to fight through all the roadblocks and to persevere. When you are inspired, you are able to take charge of the day and ultimately have a beneficial value to whatever you are meant to do or be.

Finally, when you create, build, love, innovate, volunteer, or make a positive impact, then you are creating lasting memories. You also may be more inclined to focus on taking care of your holistic health, both mind and body. If you continue to do so, then you are building your life story and adding to your ultimate legacy. Health and legacy planning will be the main focus in the next two sections.

# Focused Directions

*The pessimist complains about the wind; the optimist expects it to change; the realist adjusts the sails.* (William Arthur Ward)

*Where there's hope, there's life. It fills us with fresh courage and makes us strong again.* (Anne Frank)

*Do the best you can until you know better. Then when you know better, do better.* (Maya Angelou)

*Don't underestimate the power of vision and direction. These are irresistible forces, able to transform what might appear to be unconquerable obstacles into traversable pathways and expanding opportunities.* (Jordan Peterson)

*Your vision will become clear when you can look into your own heart. Who looks outside, dreams; who looks inside, awakes.* (Carl Jung)

*The only impossible journey is the one you never begin.* (Tony Robbins)

*One always has enough time, if one will apply it well. (Johann* Wolfgang Von Goethe)

*Efforts and courage are not enough without purpose and direction.* (John F. Kennedy)

*During my long life, I have learned one lesson: that the most important thing is to realize why one is alive—and I think it is not only to build bridges or tall buildings or make money; but to do something truly important, to do something for humanity. To bring joy, hope, to make life richer for the spirit because you have been alive, that is the most important thing.* (Arthur Rubinstein)

# PART 2

## Your Health
### (Maximizing each day)

# CHAPTER 9

# Stay Healthy

*A healthy person has a thousand wishes, but a sick person has only one.* (Indian proverb)

Do you want to stay healthy? Yes, of course. Obviously, everyone does. The bigger question is: How much are you willing to work to acquire exceptional health and then maintain it? It takes discipline, planning, and energy to achieve this target. It takes good habits and routines to maintain it. When you are healthier and are operating on all cylinders, you are better prepared to accomplish more in life.

Think about it this way. Let's say you are on an airplane that begins to taxi out to the runway. You will then hear the flight attendants go through their preflight mandatory ritual of safety instructions just in case something goes wrong during the flight. One of the instructions they cover is in the event of cabin pressure loss. If that should occur, then emergency oxygen masks would drop down from panels above the seat. Passengers are then instructed to place the mask over their nose and mouth first before helping others.

The same principle applies to you. You must take care of your own health before you can be of use to others. This means that your physical, mental, and emotional capacity should be working in sync. The healthier you are, the more energy you have to help others. There are fewer distractions, and you are more apt to remain focused on whatever task you are working on. The longer you can stay healthy, the more quality time you have to enjoy your life. When you are able to eat healthy, exercise routinely, sleep regularly, and manage your stress levels, there are wonderful rewards. You will feel better, enthusiastic, confident, and passionate about life.

Everyone would acknowledge that there are things beyond your control and that life can change quickly. There is an element of luck as health and welfare can be compromised through no fault of your own. Some things are unavoidable. Accidents, illnesses, and diseases are always a possibility. There will always be challenges ahead. It is at times like these that your attitude matters. Stay as positive as you can. Do what you can to get healthier. Seek professional help if needed. Keep your chin up. Your family, faith, and community can also provide comfort and the strength to help you through a rough patch or a health emergency.

While no one can be completely prepared for every twist and turn that life brings, there are some basic tenets that can help you on an everyday basis so that you and your body are able to react and respond to whatever curves come your way.

So what are these basic tenets? I already stated this above. In a nutshell, they are sleep, eat, move, stay mentally sharp, and manage your stress. Sounds simple, right? Nothing newsworthy here because it's common sense. Saying, believing, and doing are not necessarily connected. Being consistent is challenging as well. Life happens and gets in the way. This includes work, family, financial concerns, health, anger, guilt, fear, or other factors. Sometimes all you need is a reminder mechanism to center yourself and start again. It's your life. Make the commitment. The wonderful benefits of good health are worth the effort. Stay with it even if you falter. Never give up. Instead, just start over. You can do it. The basics of staying healthy are the focal point of this section of the book.

# Interesting Reflections

*Sorry, there's no magic bullet. You gotta eat healthy and live healthy to be healthy and look healthy. End of story.*
(Morgan Spurlock)

*The first wealth is health.* (Ralph Waldo Emerson)

*Prevention is so much better than healing.* (Thomas Adams)

*Think in the morning. Act in the noon. Eat in the evening. Sleep in the night.* (William Blake)

*Love yourself enough to live a healthy lifestyle.* (Jules Robson)

*Health is not about the weight you lose, it's about the life you gain.* (Author Unknown)

*If you achieve all kinds of things in the material world, but you lose your health or your peace of mind, you get little or no pleasure from your other accomplishments.* (Brian Tracy)

*The higher your energy level, the more efficient your body. The more efficient your body, the better you feel and the more you will use your talent to produce outstanding results.* (Tony Robbins)

# CHAPTER 10

# Eat

*The food you eat can be the safest and most powerful form of medicine or the slowest form of poison.* (Ann Wigmore)

Eating healthy is a lifestyle choice. While there are many benefits to eating healthy, it is harder to sustain it in the long term. Eating healthy is important for making sure your body continues to function well. It will help to prevent against conditions such as high blood pressure, diabetes, and heart disease. It can help slow down the advancement of osteoporosis and even some forms of cancer. It helps bring vitality and energy. It improves your immune system, your mood, and your sense of well-being, and it helps you age gracefully and live longer.

Since I am not a nutritionist or dietician, nor do I pretend to be one, here are some quick general and universal reminders. While the devil is in the details, have a plan or diet that you can maintain.

- Be prudent and calculated about what you eat.
- Eat healthy most or all of the time. Cut down on unhealthy or junk food.

- Slow down and chew your food to help your digestive system.
- Don't overeat; less is better.
- Stay hydrated and drink lots of water. It has been suggested that you should drink the equivalent of half of your body weight in ounces each day. Whatever the amount is, it's healthy to stay hydrated.
- Choose your snacks carefully—make them healthier and higher quality, such as nuts and seeds.
- Diversify your food intake to include a variety of nutrients such as eating different types of vegetables.
- When you can, choose fresh foods. They have undergone less processing and are healthier. If you can afford it, make more organic choices.
- Try to avoid unhealthy cooking oils.
- Be more aware of what goes into your body such as sugar, salt, processed foods, etc. Focus on the quality of what you consume, including supplements.
- Limit refined carbs and avoid high-fructose corn syrup.
- The human body is capable of adjusting itself and healing if you take care of it.

Eating healthy has an impact on the health of your brain. A healthy diet can diminish the threats from excess glucose intake, stress, and inflammation. For those of you who want to eat healthier, start with an achievable goal. Eat healthy 50 percent of the time and over time, increase the number to say 75-80 percent (or higher) of the time. Don't feel that you need to be at 100 percent. Remember that "eating in moderation" means showing some restraint and avoiding excessive eating practices. Be more deliberate and less impulsive about what you consume. Eat to live; don't live to eat.

Another healthy suggestion is to consider intermittent fasting, which is eating with periodic time periods without meals. There are many variations of this. According to David Sinclair, Australian biologist and author of *Lifespan*:

> *Today, human studies are confirming that once-in-a-while caloric restrictions can have tremendous health results, even if the times of fasting are quite transient . . . Almost any periodic fasting diet that does not result in malnutrition is likely to put your longevity genes to work in ways that will result in a long, healthier life.* (Sinclair 2019)

On the topic of healthy eating, David Sinclair adds this advice:

> *After twenty-five years of researching aging and having read thousands of scientific papers, if there is one piece of advice I can offer, one surefire way to stay healthy longer, one thing you can do to maximize your lifespan right now, it's this: eat less often.* (Sinclair 2019)

In summary, be mindful of what you eat. If you do consume something unhealthy, enjoy it and move on. Just keep in mind the bigger picture of healthy eating and the benefits that come with it. Your food choices matter and will impact your overall long-term health. Consume a variety of foods to get enough of the important nutrients. Eat slowly, chew and digest your food carefully, and enjoy the tastes of good food as well as the fun of eating. Bon appétit!

# Savory Bites

*Moderation. Small helpings. Sample a little bit of everything. These are the secrets of happiness and well-being.* (Julia Child)

*Every time you eat is an opportunity to nourish your body.* (Author Unknown)

*Eating healthy food fills your body with energy and nutrients. Imagine your cells smiling back at you and saying: "Thank you!"* (Karen Salmansohn)

*Eat food. Not too much. Mostly plants.* (Michael Pollan)

*Fitness is 20% exercise and 80% nutrition. You can't outrun your fork.* (Author Unknown)

*Eat for nutrition and food value. Emphasize natural foods, avoid processed foods and eliminate junk entirely.* (Vince Gironda)

*I believe that parents need to make nutrition education a priority in their home environment. It's crucial for good health and longevity to instill in your children sound eating habits from an early age.* (Cat Cora)

*The lowest-hanging fruit in preventative medicine is just to focus on nutrition.* (Peter Thiel)

*Water is the most neglected nutrient in your diet, but one of the most vital.* (Julia Child)

*Drinking good wine with good food in good company is one of life's most civilized pleasures.* (Michael Broadbent)

*I can't lose any weight. I tried jogging but I keep running into restaurants.* (Rodney Dangerfield)

*I always cook with wine. Sometimes I even add it to the food.* (W. C. Fields)

# CHAPTER 11

# Exercise

*It is exercise alone that supports the spirit and keeps the mind in vigor.* (Cicero)

There are no secrets here. You already know that exercising regularly is one of the key ingredients to good health. It is not my intent to tell you how to exercise but instead to emphasize why exercising is so important and beneficial.

Most authorities suggest that the important thing to remember is to keep moving throughout the day and not be a couch potato. Exercising is personal and can mean something different to everyone. It is dependent on age, health, ability, and access to equipment or facilities. Some may like to exercise primarily outdoors and love that connectivity that outdoor sports and nature rewards you with. Others among you are self-motivated and like to do your own thing or like to work out either in a class setting or with a trainer. Decide for yourself whether you prefer walking, swimming, biking, running, other conditioning exercises, or resistance training. Just keep moving. Have a routine or a backup plan when weather conditions are not cooperating. Always make room for stretching to make sure your body is loosened up. This should be done throughout the day, as needed, but prior to any strenuous activity. Except for your daily stretching, mix up your routines to work different muscles and parts of your body.

Take care of your body and treat it well. Imagine this: When you purchase your first car, you are notified that you have to maintain and keep it for the rest of your life. There will be no option to exchange it, sell it, or buy a new vehicle. In that case, you would learn to quickly be extra careful in how you drove and cared for it. Well, now acknowledge that the same principle applies to your body and that you must maintain and care for it for as long as you live. You will want to keep your body healthy using all practical tools that are at your disposal.

So what are the real benefits of exercising? For starters, here is Chris Johnson, the founder and CEO of On Target Living:

> *Exercise has so many wonderful benefits, including improved bone health, better balance and strength, heart health, lower blood pressure, improved brain function, decreased risk of cancer and type 2 diabetes, improved mood, increased energy, better sleep—the list is long, and the return on investment is very powerful! The number one reason I like to move my body on a daily basis is how it makes me feel during and after exercise. My mind becomes clear, my body feels loose and relaxed, and I feel energized and alive.* (Johnson 2013)

According to author and meditation coach Ilchi Lee, there are some more benefits:

*Various physical phenomena occur when you exercise.
Your heart rate rises, and your blood volume per heart-
beat increases to more quickly circulate oxygen to your
muscles and eliminate toxins in your cells. Your breathing
rate increases, and your lungs expand and contract more
frequently to discharge toxins and send more oxygen into
your blood ... Your mind will really wake up and become
alert after one minute of exercise—in short, your spirit
is focused.* (Lee 2017)

Exercise improves your lungs and heart. It protects your joints,
improves your sleep, and tones your body. Individuals who exercise
regularly are healthier and age better.

David Sinclair covers exercise and aging on a cellular level. He
discusses longevity genes and a genetic feature known as telomeres.

*Yes, exercise improves blood flow. Yes, it improves lung
and heart health. Yes, it gives us bigger, stronger muscles.
But more than any of that—and indeed what is responsible
for that—is a simple thing that happens at a much smaller
scale: the cellular scale ... Individuals who exercise more—
the equivalent of at least a half hour of jogging five days a
week—have telomeres that appear to be nearly a decade
younger than those who live a sedentary life ... Exercise
turns on the genes to make us young again on a cellular
level.* (Sinclair 2019)

He adds that high-intensity interval training raises your heart
and respiration rate and generates the greatest number of health

benefits. He also states that exposing your body to cold activates longevity genes such as cold showers or baths, even for brief moments, which can have positive impacts.

While intensity matters to maximize results, regular exercise is a springboard to many of the benefits previously mentioned. Here are some more wonderful benefits as per authors Henry Emmons and David Alter:

> *... movement can act like a wonder drug for the brain. It protects brain cells from the harmful effects of oxidation; reduces inflammation throughout the body; helps normalize blood sugar; effectively treats depression; improves the ability to learn; and promotes the survival of new brain cells. It even helps normalize levels of the stress hormone cortisol and boosts the growth factors that can help you grow a bigger, healthier, better-connected brain. Movement is a wonder drug!* (Emmons and Alter 2016)

So movement/exercise is good not only for the entire body but for your brain as well. The choice is yours. Not making time to exercise is as silly as not making time to eat. Everyone wants the benefits that regular exercise has to offer; we just need to be disciplined and make the commitment to make it a routine part of our daily life. Be accountable to yourself. If it helps, use a device like a Fitbit or something similar to help keep you on track. Form good habits. Always remember that it is never too late to start. Be proactive and disciplined. The first step is to just keep moving throughout the day. The effort you make and the energy you commit will be worthwhile. You will feel better and the quality of your life will be enhanced. Carve out the time consistently to exercise. It's worth it!

## Stepping Forward

*To keep the body in good health is a duty. Otherwise we will not be able to keep our mind strong and clear.* (Buddha)

*Take care of your body. It's the only place you have to live.* (Jim Rohn)

*One of the things I do to stay healthy and fit is to make sure I exercise every single day. Aside from eating light and getting enough sleep, exercise keeps me trim and boosts my energy.* (Martha Stewart)

*Most of us think we don't have enough time to exercise. What a distorted paradigm! We don't have time not to.* (Steven Covey)

*You will never always be motivated. You have to learn to be disciplined.* (Author Unknown)

*The reason I exercise is for the quality of life I enjoy.* (Kenneth H. Cooper)

*The first time I see a jogger smiling, I'll consider it.* (Joan Rivers)

# CHAPTER 12

# Sleep

*Sleep is the golden chain that ties health and our bodies together.*
(Thomas Dekker)

A good day begins after a good night's sleep. My experience has been that having adequate sleep helps one wake up alertly and provides the energy and state of mind to attack the day. A lack of sleep does the opposite. It impacts both the mind and the body. Without adequate sleep or rest, we become less focused and think less clearly. Our senses become dulled, and our bodies start to wear down over time. While an occasional poor night's sleep is normal, having a poor night's sleep consistently is bad for your health.

Your body has an internal cycle, also known as a circadian clock, that links your body with your brain to create a sleep-wake rhythm. Think of it as a biological clock that dictates various levels of fatigue, alertness, energy, and sleepiness throughout a twenty-four-hour period. When you get enough restorative sleep, your body and your mental capacity are able to function more effectively. However, when your outside environment changes, such as from jet lag, partying too hard, working various shifts, stress, or even excess light exposure before you go to sleep, then your circadian clock may be thrown off. These types of consistent disruptions can result in insomnia or sleep disorders. It is important to align your sleep patterns with your circadian clock to maintain a stable and healthy lifestyle.

Here is Chris Johnson discussing sleep:

> *Lack of sleep destroys the mind and body. One of the fastest ways to age the human body is lack of sleep. Poor sleep can lead to many health-related problems, such as heart disease, cancer, hormonal imbalances, obesity, headaches, high blood pressure, poor digestion, imbalanced PH, inflammation, joint pain . . . The answer to our sleep problems is not more prescription medications. The answer lies within you and learning how to improve your lifestyle!* (Johnson 2013)

Matthew Kelly has some important things to add:

> *We sleep because we have to sleep. This is true. We must sleep. Sleep is essential for survival . . . We sleep to be renewed. Sleep refreshes us. Sleep energizes us. Our sleep brings rest, renewal, and energy not only to our bodies but also to our hearts, minds, and spirits. Sleep heals us from the stresses of everyday life . . . You may think sleep is sleep. Yet numerous studies have revealed that people who sleep at the same time every night are considerably healthier than those who do not. They are affected by the common colds less than one-third as many times as people who do*

*not sleep at regular hours. The incidence of depression is also significantly lower with people who sleep at regular hours.* (Kelly 1999)

Not only is too little sleep not good for you, too much sleep is not good either. You wake up fatigued either way. So, have a proper frame of mind, be disciplined, and maintain good, consistent habits. Here are a few reminders:

Make it a priority. Understand how important it is. The older you get, the more important it becomes. Parents with younger children or pets do not always have the luxury since they are woken up more frequently. However, younger people, although more resilient than older people, can still go through periods of sleep deprivation. When you are sleep deprived, your brain can be foggy, rational thinking is slower and more difficult, and you just do not feel right.

Have a regular sleep schedule. Be disciplined and condition your body to general sleep and wake-up times. Be consistent and maintain good sleep habits.

Create a good environment for sleeping that works for you. That includes proper balance of lighting/darkness, noise, room temperature, proper pillows, and a firm mattress. The bedroom and bedding need to be cleaned regularly. Consider getting an air filter or purifier to ensure that you are breathing cleaner air.

Stay properly hydrated during the day but less so in the evening, thereby reducing the number of times you wake up.

Slow deep breathing does relax your body and helps you fall and stay asleep. Meditation is another option. It can be done in many different ways. Simply stated, it is a form of concentration and relaxation. The key is to find anything that helps you clear and slow down your mind. Try repeating positive phrases in your mind when you begin the process of falling asleep.

Another variation is to attempt to mentally relax your body slowly, focusing on each body part individually from the toes working your way to your head. As you draw attention to each part, you will find yourself more relaxed and drawing deeper into a meditative state. End with relaxing your eyes and stay centered on your eyes for a longer period. You might find yourself drifting away into sleep or at least into a more relaxed state.

As in everything health-related, stress is the great equalizer. It will keep you awake or will wake you up prematurely. While there will be nights when stress is inevitable and will hamper the quality of sleep, the key is to limit those times in your life.

Remember that sleep is not a burden for you; it is a gift. Since you will generally spend somewhere between a quarter to a third of your life in bed, learn to embrace it and maximize the positive impacts it has so that each day you are renewed, energetic, refreshed, and ready to take charge of a new day.

Besides sleeping at night and perhaps taking a short midday nap (more relevant for older people), it's important to have downtime during the day. This means you could still be awake, but your mind is taking a break and is offline. Listen to the signals your brain and body are trying to tell you when you are fatigued. Take a few minutes, unwind, rejuvenate your mind, and then continue with your day.

# Sleepy Saying

*Sleep has been provided by nature to do the body's healing work, and it take seven or eight hours for this process to happen. Commit to getting at least seven to eight hours of good quality sleep every night to keep your body and hormones in balance.* (Suzanne Summers)

*It is a common experience that a problem difficult at night is resolved in the morning after the committee of sleep has worked on it.* (John Steinbeck)

*If you can't sleep, then get up and do something instead of lying there and worrying. It's the worry that gets you, not the loss of sleep.* (Dale Carnegie)

*Sleep is an investment in the energy you need to be effective tomorrow.* (Tom Roth)

*When I woke up this morning my girlfriend asked me, "Did you sleep good?" I said, "No, I made a few mistakes."* (Steven Wright)

## CHAPTER 13

# Stimulate Your Brain

*I like nonsense. It wakes up the brain cells.* (Dr. Seuss)

If you continuously stimulate and challenge your brain, you will help keep it healthy. When your life is filled with different mental, physical, and emotional challenges that are not destructive or overly stressful, then your brain will react in a positive manner. Brains are less effective if you do not exercise or use them properly. Your cognitive functions diminish as do your reaction time, memory, and ability to focus. When your brain is stimulated, active, and functioning well, your life improves. Brains have instinctive, emotional, compassionate, and adaptive capacities.

To understand the psychology of how the brain works and thinks, let us fall back on the wisdom of Nobel Prize-winning psychologist Daniel Kahneman, who is known for his work on the psychology of judgment as well as behavioral economics. His book *Thinking Fast and Slow* is an enlightening and classic look into how our minds work.

He defines the brain or our ability to think into fictitious categories that he calls System 1 and System 2. System 1 operates automatically and quickly with little or no effort. It is fast-thinking, emotional, on autopilot, and reactive. It is impulsive and uses reflexes. It's doing without thinking, something all of us do a countless number of times every day. System 2 allocates attention to complex thoughts and concentration. System 2 is slow-thinking, logical, and deliberate. It takes more of a cognitive effort to make decisions. Kahneman makes the case that too often we suffer mental fallacies because we are too quick to accept the information that System 1 provides for us without first analyzing it through System 2. Our brain takes shortcuts, which causes us to have errors in judgment. That is why sometimes when it comes to important decisions, it is best to not rush but rather "sleep on it."

The way to block errors is to slow down, recognize the signs that your thinking is too quick, and be more calculated in your thought process. This will help you make better decisions while exercising your brain cells at the same time.

Daniel Kahneman also has other thoughts about how we think and live. Besides "2 systems," he describes "2 selves." The first is the experiencing self (similar to System 1), which does the living and makes choices. The experiencing self lives in the moment and creates memories. Logically, the experiencing self can be defined as a series of moments, each with an intrinsic value attached to it. Then there is the remembering self (similar to System 2), which tells stories that are represented by a few critical moments, which he calls the "peak end rule." In other words, we tend to remember the best and worst moments more than anything else as well as the last experience. The remembering self typically ignores the duration of a memory, or how long something lasts, either good or bad. This can distort our reflections of the actual experience. Our memories are not always accurate and are subject to bias, in regards to what we can retrieve from a few distinct memories we have.

Why is all this important? Because this explains a lot about how your brain makes decisions and how your memory operates. System 1 and System 2 are just simplistic characterizations that remind you that sometimes you need to slow down, think more, and analyze your options in order to make better decisions. The same depiction applies to the two selves. You must not be too hard on yourself if you cannot always recall details—say, of a vacation. You are not alone. During your vacation, you lived in the moment, but years later, you will most likely recall the highlights or lowlights but not necessarily many moments in between.

A healthy brain is also a curious brain: curiosity to learn more, to seek what is new and interesting. It is a state of mind that challenges you to go beyond what you already know, to stretch and exercise your brain. In essence, it helps reboot your brain. Curiosity then leads to creativity. Here is more insight on the importance of staying curious from Henry Emmons and David Alter:

> *If your mind is curiosity-driven, then your brain is continuously expanding, modifying, and reconstituting its network of neural connections. In short, the commitment to becoming a lifelong learner is an important factor in keeping the brain young and flexible ... a curious mind gathers new experiences that add to our storehouse of accumulated knowledge and wisdom.* (Emmons and Alter 2016)

Like anything else, even curiosity has limitations and can be counterproductive if it is not channeled properly. An example of this might be obsessing over someone or something, which could lead to unnecessary chatter, jealousy, or gossip.

A youthful and healthy brain remains optimistic, which is a core element for happiness. When life brings obstacles and setbacks, optimists do not give up. Sometimes a leap of faith is needed as optimists find other ways to try again. A healthy brain is empathetic to what others are feeling. Being empathetic or compassionate allows for a more intimate connection to another human being. By keeping your brain vibrant, active, and stimulated, the numerous benefits include a healthier, fulfilling conscious mind with more memorable yet meaningful capacity.

# Cerebral Sentiments

*The brain is like a muscle. When it is in use, we feel very good. Understanding is joyous.* (Carl Sagan)

*The emotional brain responds to an event more quickly than the thinking brain.* (Daniel Goleman)

*Curiosity is one of the permanent and certain characteristics of a vigorous mind.* (Samuel Johnson)

*Our minds influence the key activity of the brain, which then influences everything; perception, cognition, thoughts and feelings, personal relationships; they're all a perception of you.* (Deepak Chopra)

*The most important thing is not to stop questioning. Curiosity has its own reason for existing.* (Albert Einstein)

*I've got the brain of a four-year-old. I'll bet he was glad to get rid of it.* (Groucho Marx)

*Curiosity killed the cat, but for a while I was a suspect.* (Steven Wright)

# CHAPTER 14

# De-stress

*Instead of worrying about what could go wrong, change your thoughts to what can go right. When you change the negative thought into a positive one, it eliminates the negative one.*
(Roy T. Bennett)

You can be doing everything right. You are eating healthy, exercising regularly, sleeping at regular intervals, keeping your brain active, and overall living a healthy lifestyle. However, too much stress for an extended period of time can negate all the good work and effort that you do. Too much stress will make you age and possibly lead to other physical or mental issues. It can subtract from your happiness, enjoyment, and quality and love of life.

Having some stress in your life is needed to perform at a higher level. It helps get your attention and stimulates you to focus on the task at hand. For example, many people get nervous before making an important speech. That's a normal good type of stress. A certain type and amount of stress is a key ingredient to maximizing your performance levels. Finding that balance is important, as Chris Johnson points out:

*You need enough stress to challenge you and make you grow, but not too much that you can't keep up and stress is breaking you down. Finding that "right" balance of stress and gaining the skills necessary to control your mind is critical for your success in business, your personal life, and your health and well-being!* (Johnson 2013)

Having bad days or bad moments are a part of life. You won't be able to avoid it. No one can. These events or periods in your life can occur abruptly without any warning. Some of these events can be traumatic and can cause acute stress, or something that is temporary and lasts for a short period of time. Your body reacts, such as when you perceive danger, and then it reverts back to normal. This is healthy and normal stress.

Chronic stress is different and is unhealthy and abnormal. It is when your body and mind are constantly exposed or consumed with negative outcomes about people, places, and many aspects of your life. This type of negative obsession creates anxiety and many other accompanying emotions such as fear, depression, and apprehension. Anxiety brings uneasiness and distress. There are many natural ways to combat chronic stress. The first step is to recognize what is causing it. Take some time to step back and analyze the root cause. Then figure out what necessary changes are needed to reduce or eliminate the pressures in your life that are creating your negative stress. Here are some other common-sense stress management ideas:

- Stretch out and then take a walk. Any good form of exercise will help.

- Talk through your anxiety with someone you trust.
- Take a deep breath and count to ten. This will pump in oxygen and give you some relief. (See Chapter 15 for the 4-7-8 technique.)
- Meditation is another form of relaxation therapy.
- Relaxation, smiling, and laughter work well to reduce stress.
- Help others deal with their own problems. It can be cathartic to help others work through their issues.
- Your strong connection to your faith and more frequent praying can be mentally and spiritually beneficial when life gets rough and tough.
- Go outside and enjoy nature. This can change your outlook and your stress levels.
- Watch your diet and your alcohol intake when your stress levels are high. Don't use wine or unnecessary drugs as an excuse to treat your state of mind; it only masks your real condition. Drink modestly only after you are in a more relaxed state.
- Find some good hobbies that you enjoy doing and use these to direct your mind away from anything stress-related.
- Finally (I like this idea since I've used it myself), go into a private room or your car and let out a primal scream at the top of your lungs. Believe it or not, it works and feels quite therapeutic and liberating.

Here are some additional thoughts from author Skye Girard:

*You can also invent your own stress management tips. The basic idea is to identify the cause of stress and to pull out from it for a moment and then deal with it . . . Drinking a glass of water or playing small games are simple stress management techniques. The whole idea is to change the focus of attention and when you return to the problem, it does not feel as monstrous as you felt before.* (Girard 2015)

The main takeaway is that you must find ways to help you cope with any form of chronic or acute stress. If your mind and body are already healthy, you will find yourself more resilient to stress. Nevertheless, if your stress levels are elevated, either try one of the suggestions above or find something that will lift your spirits.

As a last resort, if your chronic stress is too overwhelming, seek professional help. Here are a few warning signs as to when professional help may be warranted:

- Mental signs may include massive mood swings, depression, panic attacks, inability to focus, and changes in behavior or in personality.
- Physical signs may include but are not limited to large weight fluctuations, exhaustion, persistent aches and pains, sleep issues, digestive issues, or heart or blood pressure problems.
- Stress impacts the outlook and quality of life as well as job performance and relationships.

The bottom line is that you must pay attention to the stress in your life, and what is causing it, and be proactive in your approach to mitigate it. You must effectively manage your stress before it effectively manages you.

# Stress Busters

*For every minute you remain angry, you give up sixty seconds of peace of mind.* (Ralph Waldo Emerson)

*The greatest weapon against stress is our ability to choose one thought over another.* (William James)

*Thankfulness can reduce stress in your life by making you more content with who you are and what you have. If you make a habit of accepting every circumstance gracefully and assuming there is a purpose in it, you'll be relieved from the worry and anxiety that go with being resentful and dissatisfied.* (Thomas Kinkade)

*In times of great stress or adversity, it's always best to keep busy, to plow your anger and your energy into something positive.* (Lee Iacocca)

*If you ask what the single most important key to longevity is, I would have to say it is avoiding worry, stress, and tension. And if you didn't ask me, I'd still have to say it.* (George Burns)

## CHAPTER 15

# Breathe and Meditate

*The greatest weapon against stress is relaxed breathing.*
(Amit Ray)

All of us breathe without any conscious effort, as it comes naturally. It is congruent with Daniel Kahneman's System 1 (comes automatically, like being on autopilot). Most of the time, that is quite sufficient, but how you breathe can make a difference when you are managing acute or chronic stress. During these times, you need to slow down and concentrate more on your breathing. You need to breathe slowly and deeply. In doing so, your outlook might improve as your mind, body, and soul are calmer and more synchronized. Always remember to just breathe deeply when you are feeling a little overwhelmed.

Deep breathing is a valuable tool when you are attempting to maximize personal performance levels. For example, before taking an exam, giving a presentation, competing in sporting events, etc., it helps to slow your mind down and stay focused on the tasks at hand.

Breathing is powerful. It can provide a path for you to let go of guilt and pain. It gives you some space to live. It helps in healing and calming yourself down. Sometimes you should take some deep breaths, clear your thoughts, and let your mind have a quick break from the issues at hand. It also is useful for when we hit a brick wall and are out of fresh ideas. First pause, close your eyes, take some deep breaths, and try to push forward one step at a time.

Here are some breathing tips from well-known doctor and author Andrew Weil:

> *Some general principles of breathwork are: make your breathing slower, deeper, quieter, and more regular whenever you think about it; deepen the exhalation phase of breathing by squeezing more air out of the lungs at the end of each breath . . . and keep your attention on the breath . . .* (Weil 2005)

Andrew Weil promotes the 4-7-8 breathing technique to help produce a relaxed state of consciousness. While there are instant positive dividends, he believes that consistent practice is the key for tangible longer-term benefits in all types of environments, those that are either stressful or stress-free. The exercise is simple and goes like this:

- Keep your tongue behind the upper front teeth and hold it during the inhale. Let it then go to where it is most comfortable during the exhale.
- Exhale through your mouth while making a "whoosh" sound.
- Inhale through your mouth to a count of four.
- Hold your breath for a count of seven.

- Open your mouth and exhale to a count of eight, making the same "whoosh" sound.
- Do this four times in a sitting and do this at least twice a day or as needed to combat anxiety or stress.

Meditation is another method for reducing stress and anxiety, stabilizing your mind, and creating positive emotions. When you meditate, you are engaging your mind in order to either contemplate, reflect on, or reach a higher degree of spiritual awareness and relaxation. Using and repeating a mantra, which can be a word, sound, or phrase, can help keep your mind in focus. Soothing spa music can also be an effective tool to steady the mind during meditation

The process of meditating, if done properly, calms your mind, thoughts, and emotions. You can meditate while sitting down or even walking. Decision-making is easier when your mind is tranquil and clear.

More from Andrew Weil:

*Meditation is nothing more than focused attention, directed inward or outward—to the breath, for instance, which is probably the most natural object of meditation, or to an external visual focus or a silently spoken word or phrase.* (Weil 2005)

Visualization is another type of relaxation and meditative technique. It is a form of daydreaming in which you imagine actual places and experiences where you have been that have given you some peace of mind, serenity, and joy. You then picture yourself in that scene or location, making your senses aware of your surroundings as you consciously find yourself becoming more relaxed.

Author and Rabbi Daniel Cohen writes about the importance of seizing meditative moments:

> *The secret to seizing meditative moments emerges from the belief that we each possess within us an inner voice, compass, and guide that reflects a higher power and purpose . . . It's the "still, small voice" that is strong and resonant, calling on us to pursue what is right and purposeful in our lives.* (Cohen 2017)

My interpretation of this excerpt is that if you get into a meditative mode by slowing your breathing down and decluttering your mind, then your mind can wander in places that either enhance your creativity or lead you upward and onward.

Breathing is naturally an extension of life. However, it becomes more of a stress reduction or protection strategy when everyday stress is enhanced. As we pointed out in the last chapter there are various techniques to diminish the threat from excessive stress or anxiety. Remember to practice and apply these techniques, particularly when you feel a panic attack starting. For example, use stress reduction or breathing techniques if you or a loved one are going through a health scare. Recognize that most health scares are either nothing or are treatable. Under these circumstances, your mind can be your biggest enemy as it goes through the worst-case scenarios. Stay in control of your mind, be positive, and try not to let it dominate your thoughts.

If you can remember anything in this chapter, it is this. When you are troubled or in emotional distress, first recognize it, then slow down and breathe calmly. Be careful not to say something impulsively that you might regret later. Walk away for a few minutes, if you need to, and either meditate or close your eyes. It will help ease your tension, reduce your heart rate and blood pressure, and clear your mind. Then you will be in a better state of mind to tackle the issues that are causing your distress.

## Deep Breaths

*When you arise in the morning, think of what a precious privilege it is to be alive—to breathe, to think, to enjoy, to live.* (Marcus Aurelius)

*Mindfulness is the moment-to-moment realization that every moment is a blessing, and every breath is divine.* (Amit Ray)

*Stop. Take three deep breaths and smile everywhere in your body, observing what is happening to your body. Proceed now with kindness and understanding.* (Deepak Chopra)

*Every day is a new beginning. Take a deep breath. Smile and start again.* (Author Unknown)

*Breathing in, I calm my body. Breathing out, I smile. Dwelling in the present moment, I know this is a wonderful moment.* (Thich Nhat Hanh)

*The way you breathe is the way you live. Breathing is essential to life and necessary for good health.* (Heidi Morrison)

*Sometimes you just have to stop, take a deep breath, and put things in perspective.* (Katrina Mayer)

*Take a deep breath and enjoy your life.* (Author Unknown)

*Mindful meditation has been discovered to foster the ability to inhibit those very quick emotional impulses.* (Daniel Goleman)

# CHAPTER 16

# Laugh

*Laughter is an instant vacation.* (Milton Berle)

While these are serious topics and serious times we live in, we should always make time to laugh. Why? It makes us feel good and is fun. There is even a genuine therapeutic aspect of laughter as it has a positive impact on both mental and physical health. Some say that it is one of the cheapest forms of medicine as it reduces stress, lowers blood pressure, increases oxygen intake, and is healthy for your heart. Laughter triggers neurotransmitters like dopamine, which acts like an antidepressant. It is also good for your brain. It makes you happy and lifts your spirits. Good humor is like the best natural miracle drug. It spreads through your veins like an infusion of happiness.

In his book *Anatomy of an Illness as Perceived by the Patient*, journalist, author, professor, and activist Norman Cousins writes about surviving a serious sudden onset illness that crippled him. After starting with traditional treatments, he became engaged in his own care and eventually recovered fully using a combination of exercise, vitamins, good nutrition, and laughter. He found that a good bout of belly laughter each day reduced his pain levels and helped in the healing process. He elaborates on the role of laughter in the following passage:

> *Immanuel Kant, in his* Critique of Pure Reason, *wrote that laughter produces a "feeling of health through the furtherance of the vital bodily processes, the affection that moves the intestines and the diaphragms; in a word, the feeling of health that makes up the gratification felt by us; so that we can thus reach the body through the soul and use the later as the physician of the former." If Kant was intimating in these remarks that he never knew a man who possessed the gift of hearty laughter to be burdened by constipation, I can heartily agree with him. It has always seemed to me that hearty laughter is a good way to jog internally without having to go outdoors . . . it creates a mood in which the other positive emotions can be put to work, too. In short, it helps make it possible for good things to happen.* (Cousins 1979)

By his own admission, Norman Cousin's unorthodox way of treatment in his case may appear to be somewhat anecdotal. It could be an outlier or an isolated case. However, the bigger point is to recognize the positive role that a proper attitude coupled with laughter could have on improving mental and physical health, both as a preventative measure and during recovery.

In his book *Laughter Therapy*, author Ace McCloud amplifies on the importance of being around people who make you laugh, as a form of therapy:

*Sigmund Freud would recommend to his depressed patients to surround themselves with people who made them laugh. If you hang around someone with a similar sense of humor, you'll be more likely to find many more things funny and laughter will come that much more easily. Also, laughter is contagious. Just being in the same room with people laughing in it can start you up.* (McCloud 2017)

Laughter can also be used as a mechanism to make a difficult past easier to cope with. Here is Ace McCloud again:

*Being able to laugh at a situation from the past has been shown to be very healing to a variety of different people. The goal is to de-sensitize the painful memory so that you don't keep constantly bringing it up, and if you do, you now remember it as a less painful or as a learning experience . . . Psychologists not only use humor to help those overcome an unhappy childhood, but new studies have shown that laughter helps survival rates in cancer patients and people undergoing organ transplants. Although the reasons for its positive psychological effects is still being speculated on, it has been clear for thousands of years that humor is good for the heart, body, and spirit . . . remember that no situation or condition is permanent—everything is subject to change; remind yourself that when you're dealing with tough situations, make a joke of it, transform the memory in your mind, and learn to laugh and smile about it!"* (McCloud 2017)

Laughter does make for good dinner conversation. Let's face it, would you rather talk about all the ills of politics, cancer, disease, debt, inflation, taxes, nuclear disarmament, everything bad in the world, or something that makes you laugh? Not that these topics aren't important—of course they are—but laughter is more enjoyable and entertaining.

Laughter can come in various forms. It can be a funny story or lines from a book, movie, television show, song, or news event (sidebar: not every news story is depressing). It can be a person, an impersonation, a remark, good-natured sarcasm, or just a joke. As stated earlier but worth repeating, sometimes just the act of laughing is contagious and causes others to laugh.

I love good humor and embrace it as an everyday part of my life. Besides this chapter, you may have noticed some comedic quotes sprinkled throughout this book. Humor has become part of who I am. It is also an excellent icebreaker and a way to bring people together. After all, who doesn't like a good laugh? During Covid, we started to add comedy to our repertoire as we were writing and sending out blast emails to our clients analyzing the economy and the markets. A little laughter was added just to take the edge off. People kept feeding us jokes and cartoons, which we just recirculated back into our reports. Although the material was not original, the intent was to make people smile, chuckle, and hopefully pay attention to the more important content.

I do want to make the following point. In my world and in my opinion, not all comedy is equal. I screen any spontaneous quips, sarcasm, jokes, videos, one-liners, or other material that I use either in person or in writing. My intent is to know my audience and to never intentionally be mean-spirited, offensive, controversial, or condescending. My goal is to be funny but to not cross the line. I also know that some remarks sound funnier in my head than when they come out of my mouth. That comes with the territory. No one is going to always be funny all of the time. However, my feeling is that if I can make someone laugh here and there and entertain them, it will make them feel good at that moment in time, which is good enough for me.

Laughing is good for your mood, emotions, and health, and it helps you connect with others. It provides common ground in a world that is becoming more and more divided. It can help you see the ridiculous aspects of everyday life and cope with negativity and misfortunes. Aside from peace and love, everyone could always use more laughter. It can brighten up your mood and spirit at any moment in time. It will make you smile, which is healthy and wholesome. So lighten up and laugh more! Incorporate levity into your life on a consistent basis. Don't be afraid to be funny. Share your comic ability and sharpen your delivery to amuse the people you are with. Remember that not every line works. Sometimes people laugh with you and sometimes they laugh at you. Don't take it personally. Be silly and then try again. Say more funny things if you are in the mood. Make it funny! Make them laugh!

# Laughing Matters

*We sleep in separate rooms, we have dinner apart, we take separate vacations. We're doing everything we can to keep our marriage together.* (Rodney Dangerfield)

*When I read about the evils of drinking, I gave up reading.* (Henny Youngman)

*Everybody laughs the same in every language because laughter is a universal connection.* (Yakov Smirnoff)

*Laughter is a tranquilizer with no side effects.* (Arnold H. Glasow)

*I used to work in a fire hydrant factory. You couldn't park anywhere near the place.* (Steven Wright)

*I finished a big book the other day. 421 pages. That's a lot of coloring when you think about it.* (Adam Sandler)

*Celebrate your success and find humor in your failures. Don't take yourself so seriously. Loosen up and everyone around you will loosen up. Have fun and always show enthusiasm. When all else fails put on a costume and sing a silly song.* (Sam Walton)

*My only regret in life is that I am not someone else.* (Woody Allen)

*There is nothing in the world so irresistibly contagious as laughter and good humor.* (Charles Dickens)

*I'm sick of following my dreams, man. I'm just going to ask where they're going and hook up with 'em later.* (Mitch Hedberg)

*Laughter helps you put everything into perspective.* (Jim Henson)

*If aliens are watching us through telescopes, they're going to think the dogs are the leaders of the planet. If you see two life forms, one of them is making a poop, the other one's carrying it for him, who would you assume is in charge?* (Jerry Seinfeld)

*I almost had a psychic girlfriend, but she left me before we met.* (Steven Wright)

(NOTE: This next Henny Youngman joke has my favorite punch line ever. In fact, when people ask me this question, I often respond with this line.)

*A man gets hit by a car while crossing the street. Another man sees him, rushes over, takes his own jacket off, rolls it up, and puts it behind the man's head who is lying on the ground. The good Samaritan asks, "Are you comfortable?" The man on the ground responds, "I make a nice living."*

## CHAPTER 17

# Watch Your Emotions

*I don't want to be at the mercy of my emotions. I want to use them. To enjoy them, and to dominate them.* (Oscar Wilde)

Experiencing different emotions is a part of everyday life. In fact, you could experience combinations of different emotions and not completely be aware of what you are feeling. The main takeaway is that you must learn to control extreme emotions and keep them in check in order to thrive, succeed, and truly enjoy life. Extreme emotions lead to higher levels of stress. You do not want or need any demons living in your head. They can act as a deterrence for exercising common sense. Even positive emotions such as happiness, joy, and excitement can be problematic, if they lead to overconfidence or if not properly correlated to reality. An example of this may include thinking that your strong feelings toward another person are automatically reciprocated, when, in reality, the feelings are not mutual. Another example may be excitement over a school or work project that you completed, only to be let down later. These feelings, if not balanced, can take you down a dark rabbit hole of negative emotions.

In her book *How to Control Your Emotions*, author Jennifer Smith writes:

> *Not all emotions we face every day are happy ones; in fact, most people are riddled with negative emotions through-out the day. In most cases, negative emotions such as fear, anxiety, anger, frustration, sadness, shame, and guilt overrule the positive emotions. It becomes almost impos-sible to be a happy person if we pay too much attention to the negative ones or let them control our lives. If we are constantly in a bad mood, angry about all the injustice in the world, frustrated about not being able to succeed or sad about a personal loss, our lives will become intolerable. It will be impossible to live a full life if we are constantly focusing on our negative emotions and letting them rule our lives . . . If we let our emotions take a control on us, we can never learn to control them and be a happier person.* (Smith 2021)

Emotions such as guilt, jealousy, and anger are destructive forms of consciousness if they dominate your thoughts. They crowd out and limit your potential for growth and happiness. It is toxic to your health if left unchecked because strong emotions can lead to bad decision-making. In essence, your pessimism changes the essence of who you once were. Optimists tend to do better in life than pessimists. They achieve more and are genuinely happier.

Being aware of your negative emotions while they are occurring is a good first step. In other words, be mindful and in the moment. There is an expression that it's hard to watch a movie when you are in it. True, but it can still be done. Be careful if you lose your temper. Watch what you say out loud because you may regret it later. Calm down quickly. Be flexible enough to give yourself an emotional off-ramp.

Sometimes you need to clear the air and let your emotions out. This helps you unclutter your mind and reset yourself. When you feel the need to do this, diffuse the anger and guilt, be kind to yourself afterward, and try to lower your emotional temperature. Lose the resentment, frustration, and hostility in your mind and let your emotions wind down.

Picture this analogy in your mind. When you are driving a car, you are typically in total control of the speed, direction, climate, sound system, destination, and overall driving experience. Let's say you are driving while in a stable and normal emotional state of mind. Then someone else enters the car. It is your extreme emotions (your alter ego) who join you in the passenger seat. Do not relinquish control of the car over to this troublemaker and allow this dark passenger to interfere with the ride, or your life. Your irrational emotional alter ego is not in any condition to operate a vehicle at optimum capacity and could inflict potentially serious damage or cause an accident, negatively impacting both others and yourself. You have the ability and means of remaining in charge since you are the driver of the car; your emotions, attitude, and life choices. Pay attention to your environment and stay in control of your emotions.

Andrew Weil writes about the strategy of substituting other emotions to replace negative emotions:

*Once you are aware of habits of thought that lead to nega-*
*tive emotions, you can begin to substitute other ones. For*

*example, whenever you notice yourself ruminating on a theme like I am worthless and this latest setback just confirms it, you can consciously substitute This setback is just something that happened; I will get through it because I am capable and resilient. The theory behind this work is simple: it is impossible to hold opposite thoughts in mind at the same time, and the impact of a negative thought on feeling can be canceled by thinking a positive one. As you practice the substitution of positive thinking for negative thinking, it will gradually become the dominant habit.* (Weil 2005)

What he is saying is that while you may not be able to stop negative thinking or images, learning to identify what produces those emotions, then substituting those with images that emit happier emotions, is an effective strategy for improving your mental health. When you are in control of your emotions, you have more control over the direction of your life. While it takes discipline, restraint, and fortitude, the upside is tremendous. By doing so, it will provide you with a better opportunity to lead a healthier and balanced lifestyle.

Here are the main points of this chapter:

- Be aware of your emotions and what is driving your emotions to be elevated.
- You have the power to consciously choose how to control your emotions. There are techniques to de-stress that were covered in this chapter as well as Chapters 14 and 15.
- Stay in or regain control of extreme emotions as they arise.
- You cannot always control a situation, but what you can control is how you respond to it emotionally.

# Emotional Checks and Balances

*We either make ourselves miserable or we make ourselves strong. The amount of work is the same.* (Carlos Castaneda)

*Human behavior flows from three main sources: desire, emotion, and knowledge.* (Plato)

*Keeping your emotions in check gives you the advantage.* (Leandra De Andrade)

*In order to move on, you must understand why you felt what you did and why you no longer need to feel it.* (Mitch Albom)

*If your emotional abilities aren't in hand, if you don't have self-awareness, if you are not able to manage your distressing emotions, if you can't have empathy and have effective relationships, then no matter how smart you are, you are never going to get very far.* (Daniel Goleman)

*The feeling is a natural process, and it can't be faked. Everybody has the same feeling in most situations. Emotions are the expressions you want to show the world, no matter how you feel inside.* (Author Unknown)

*Take control of your consistent emotions and begin to consciously and deliberately reshape your daily experience of life.* (Tony Robbins)

*(When you are upset, or your emotions are triggered) Just let the emotions and thoughts pass like clouds in the sky.*
(Patricia Angus)

*Don't sweat the petty things and don't pet the sweaty things.*
(George Carlin)

# CHAPTER 18

# Be Present

*The ability to be in the present moment is a major component of mental wellness.* (Abraham Maslow)

Have you ever been to a prize drawing where the sponsor picks the winning ticket, but with the caveat that you must be present to win? That also applies to living your best life on a daily basis. Being present is one of the most important factors when it comes to connecting with others. This means being fully engaged when you are conversing.

It's important to be in the moment, to listen carefully, to pay attention, and to be there mentally. If you are with someone in person, then it means making good eye contact, being aware of your body language, and maintaining good posture. When you are able to focus your attention in the moment, your communication skills grow. In addition, other people are more attentive, respectful, and receptive to you. As you are probably aware, always being present is easier said than done. You are living in an era of complexity, interruptions, and distractions. You are frequently multitasking and paying more attention to your issues, problems, and desires.

As a result, your mind wanders elsewhere. Information flows at a high velocity, which sometimes can be overwhelming. When you find this happening, simply slow down, breathe, and refocus your attention.

Going back to Daniel Kahneman and his description of the two fictional systems and two selves, there are times we need to engage System 2 (think slow) and override our automatic response that System 1 (think fast) brings with it. The objective is to shift your attention to more deliberate thought and concentration. In this capacity, our experiencing self can be fully engaged in the moment and closely committed to the here and now. Employing System 2 will enhance your capacity to remember (your remembering self) what took place, at a later time.

Being present is about paying attention. In their book *Staying Sharp* authors Henry Emmons and Davis Alter quote Buddhist monk Thich Nhat Hanh:

*The most precious gift we can offer anyone is our attention.*

They then continue with the following insight:

*This is what is known as* mindfulness—*the ability to remain present from moment to moment on purpose, through the power of intention. It sounds simple and it is. But there is enough subtlety and nuance to it that you could practice mindfulness your whole life and still grow in your ability to be more present. And that would be a very worthy life's pursuit!* (Emmons and Alter 2016)

Being present has other health attributes. It activates and exercises your brain since your mind is not wandering off. It brings awareness and ultimately increases your level of confidence, and happiness. It brings clarity with fewer redundancies.

To quote author and mental health expert Ken Druck:

*Our greatest challenge and opportunity is in living in the gratitude and the grace of this fleeting, eternal moment. Life is not something that's going to happen. It's something right here right now! A life of integrity and meaning begins with being present and showing up in the moment of one's own life. Moment after moment.* (Druck 2013)

Daniel Cohen reflects upon the power of one moment:

*Moments are as numerous as the stars in the sky, and any one of them could prove to be the most significant of our lives . . . Realizing that any moment can be one of growth is the first step. Be receptive . . . Being present is one of the most powerful tools you'll discover in life . . . When you're speaking to someone, be fully engaged. When you're outside, be fully present in the beauty of the moment.* (Cohen 2017)

He continues with an astute thought:

*Listen closely to a secret I'm about to share. It will transform the way you live and the way you'll be remembered:* We don't remember days, we remember moments. (Cohen 2017)

Our ability to be present, to be there, to be in the moment is an art that must be practiced, maintained, and refined. When you are distracted or having trouble focusing, try to remind yourself that life is happening right now and that you need to be present.

- Be there for your loved ones and for yourself.
- Remind yourself that life is precious and it is short.
- Live in the present.
- Listen and let others talk.
- Enjoy and embrace each moment as it comes and it goes.

# Precious Moments

*You must live in the present, launch yourself on every wave, find your eternity in each moment.* (Henry David Thoreau)

*Sometimes you will never know the value of a moment until it becomes a memory.* (Dr. Seuss)

*The present moment, though fleeting, is the only tangible moment. The rest are a heap of memories.* (Michael Bassey Johnson)

*Don't let yesterday use up too much of today.* (Will Rogers)

*Remember then: there is only one time that is important—Now! It is the most important time because it is the only time when we have any power.* (Leo Tolstoy)

*Be present in all things and be thankful for all things.* (Maya Angelou)

*The past is a place of reference, not a place of residence; the past is a place of learning, not a place of living.* (Roy T. Bennett)

*Life gives you plenty of time to do whatever you want to do if you stay in the present moment.* (Deepak Chopra)

*The older one gets, the more one feels that the present must be enjoyed; it is a precious gift, comparable to a state of grace.* (Marie Curie)

*I just got one last thing. I urge all of you, all of you, to enjoy your life, the precious moments you have. To spend each day with some laughter and some thought, to get your emotions going.*
(Jim Valvano)

# CHAPTER 19

# Have Balance

*Most of us spend too much time on what is urgent and not enough time on what is important.* (Stephen Covey)

When it comes to living a healthy and fulfilling life, perspective matters. Would you agree that having some order and balance in your life is a critical ingredient to managing good health? If you are working or are in school, then it's maintaining the right balance between work, leisure, family, social engagement, and maintaining a healthy lifestyle. That means working hard, playing hard, and being strategic on how you spend your time. Taking care of your physical and mental needs is a job in itself. The greater your physical and mental health is, the more successful you will be in all aspects of your life and the more pleasurable life will be. What is the right balance? That will be up to you to determine. The main point is that you need to be smart, disciplined, and proactive about managing your health. It is preferable if you can do it as naturally and organically as possible.

Maintaining good balance is akin to homeostasis, which by definition is the tendency toward a relatively stable equilibrium between different but interdependent elements. These elements include all the health-related topics covered in this section. In order to maximize your mental and physical health, it's important to remind yourself that there is a certain symmetry between how you treat your body and your overall health, as all actions have consequences, good or bad. There is also a certain synergy when you persevere and stay balanced. The reward is that it will positively impact your purpose, your health, and your legacy.

For example, a symphony orchestra is comprised of many musicians playing a variety of musical instruments. While each type of individual instrument is played independently of each other, they are interdependent in order to create perfect harmony as the sounds of the instruments are blended together. The role of the conductor is to set the tempo and coordinate the musicians, the sound, and the performance. It takes skill and lots of practice for an orchestra to come together and make beautiful music. If an instrument is either out of tune or out of beat, then that impacts the sound quality and thus the overall audience experience.

The same holds true if you are out of tune or out of beat with your body or your life. It takes discipline and desire to stay on the right course. If you eat well, sleep well, and exercise, but cannot control your stress or emotions, then you are out of balance and may be susceptible to greater long-term health risks. Treat your mind and body well and be cautious of avoiding extreme abnormal behaviors that are detrimental to your health, such as drinking too much or other compulsive vices.

If you are retired, you still need to maintain a sense of balance between staying healthy and performing essential tasks, activities, and hobbies and meeting social commitments. As you continue to age, focusing on maintaining a healthy lifestyle and balance should be one of your daily priorities. Just continue to eat as well as possible, move, rest, exercise your brain, and manage your stress, anxieties, and emotions. Don't always take life seriously and laugh more. Be present and live in the moment.

When your life is balanced, you are typically more cognizant of your body's needs and the warning signs when things are off a bit. You are all going to go through days or periods when your energy levels are down, you are not feeling 100 percent, or you are lacking confidence or self-assurance; days when your rhythm is off, you don't have time to exercise or rest properly, and your anxiety is heightened. That's perfectly normal. Allow yourself some space to recover and then start over. Remind yourself to keep your head up, breathe, stay calm, and keep your wits about you. Don't let things frazzle you. Tomorrow is another day; you can reset yourself to get back to a properly balanced lifestyle.

Making wise daily decisions to increase the probability of staying healthy is the most important gift you can grant yourself. Although there are never any guarantees in life, it's prudent to put yourself in the best position for a successful outcome. When you are healthy and working on all cylinders, you are in a better position to maximize your skills for work or pleasure. You are also better prepared to live your life to the fullest degree and to achieve your goals.

So having balance is key. Keep in mind the old adage that states that everything in moderation is the secret to life, even when you part from the normal course of your daily routines. Stay disciplined but cut yourself some slack and allow some flexibility, when needed.

When you are indeed as healthy as possible, both physically and mentally, you will be well equipped for dealing with unexpected twists and turns in your life. While good health is not necessarily a prerequisite, you will be better prepared mentally, physically, and emotionally to search and discover what your sense of purpose is. With clarity, direction, and purpose, you can then contemplate or plan for your ultimate legacy. Everything does ultimately tie in neatly together. From the determination, structure, and lifestyle you design, your life can form a natural ebb and flow. Proper lifestyle balance will keep you grounded and allow you to do much more with your life.

# Balanced Treasures

*Life is like riding a bicycle. You must keep moving to maintain the balance.* (Albert Einstein)

*Just as your car runs more smoothly and requires less energy to go faster and farther when the wheels are in perfect alignment, you perform better when your thoughts, feelings, emotions, goals, and values are in balance.* (Brian Tracy)

*The foundation stones for a balanced success are honesty, character, integrity, faith, love, and loyalty.* (Zig Ziglar)

*Balance, peace, and joy are the fruit of a successful life. It starts with recognizing your talents and finding ways to serve others by using them.* (Thomas Kinkade)

*A good stance and posture reflect a proper state of mind.* (Morihei Ueshiba)

*Work-life balance, work-life effectiveness, personal and professional satisfaction—or whatever you choose to call it—is not an entitlement or benefit. Your company cannot give it to you. You have to create it for yourself.* (Matthew Kelly)

*In between goals is a thing called life, that has to be lived and enjoyed.* (Sid Caesar)

*In therapy I learned the importance of keeping spiritual life and professional life balanced. I need to regain my balance.*
(Tiger Woods)

*Life is about balance. Be kind, but don't let people abuse you. Trust, but don't be deceived. Be content, but never stop improving yourself.* (Zig Ziglar)

CHAPTER 20

# Live Longer

*Positive people have more friends which is a key factor of
happiness and longevity.* (Robert Putnam)

Stanislaw Kowalski did not let age slow down his ambitions. He
was 105 years old when he participated in the Polish track and
field championship in 2015. He competed in the 100-meter race,
the shot put, and the discus throw.

It is a somewhat universal desire to be blessed with a long and
healthy life. Of course, there are no guarantees that on an individual
basis this will occur. With that being said, this chapter will cover
some common denominators for various groups of centurions and
how they achieved greater longevity. Explorer and author Dan
Buettner has visited areas all over the world and has discovered
pockets of communities in various countries where people are living longer, which he has labeled as Blue Zones. He has interviewed
many of these centurions, has written multiple books about them,
and is considered to be a pioneer and expert on Blue Zone research.

So what are some of the common traits for longevity? While
these habits may vary from region to region, here is a quick list

of generally what it takes to live longer, which comes from Dan's research. You will be able to connect his research to topics covered in previous chapters. The secrets are not complicated to understand, but it is challenging to implement them consistently. While you might want to make some changes in your life, don't feel like you have to change everything at once or who you are. Just make subtle changes and be the best version of yourself.

- *Be active every day*, without thinking about it. In other words, let it be a natural byproduct of your daily living with it occurring instinctively. Let it become a part of who you are. Just have fun and keep moving and do what you enjoy doing.
- *Be aware of calorie intake.* Try to lower calorie intake by a reasonable amount. There is a significant calorie difference between eating until your stomach is full and when you are no longer hungry.
- *Watch what you eat.* Limit your intake of meat and focus more on fruits, vegetables, nuts, and plant-based foods. Avoid processed foods. Fast occasionally.
- *Drink plenty of water.* Stay hydrated and drink around 5-6 glasses a day. While staying hydrated is always important, the amount consumed could vary based upon the climate, activity level, and each individual's unique circumstances.
- *Drink red wine in moderation.* His research suggests that having a daily drink or two per day (beer, wine, or other spirits too) has some positive health benefits particularly with a meal. It has positive social benefits, reduces stress, and brings friends and family together.

- *Have purpose in life.* This is obviously a foundational theme throughout this book. In Blue Zone research, having purpose reduces stress and has clear health benefits. He elaborates that purpose can come from many sources such as a job, hobby, children, grandchildren, or a new activity such as learning a musical instrument or a new language. These activities help exercise your brain and answer the question as to why you get up every morning. (See Chapter 1.)

- *Do what you can to reduce stress.* That could mean slowing down, appreciating and being with friends, making family a priority, and/or having time for serenity, meditation, and spirituality. Take short naps when needed. The goal is to reduce the noise in your life and to prioritize some quiet or fun space in your life. This also means having a greater awareness that hurrying and worrying about so many aspects of your life is sometimes not worth it or is just not that important.

- *Belong or participate in a spiritual community.* By doing so, you are less likely to make harmful or unhealthy decisions as there is a morality and code of ethics to follow in every organized religion. There appears to be a strong correlation that people with faith volunteer often to help others in need. Doing so elevates self-esteem, which has a positive health benefit and provides a heightened sense of personal satisfaction. Belonging to a religious community can shift or relinquish stress of everyday life to a higher deity or power.

- *Make family a priority.* In other words, put family first, offering love and devotion. Typically, lifelong commitments to family members are reciprocated with love and care. Family is the highest form of social networking. Having traditions, rituals, family time, and good bonding time are all important steps to help stay close.

- *Be surrounded by those who share similar healthy Blue Zone type of values.* Be connected socially with those who have common goals and similar lifestyles and you want to be with. Having good social networks is a great investment in time and energy. A strong friendship requires effort but the rewards are terrific.

- *Enjoy the simple pleasures in life.* Take in the fresh air outside on a nice day, take a walk, and focus on nature, family, God, and whatever else reduces stress. Have the right attitude; it will help you get through any hardships.

- *Be likable.* If you are likable, it is easier to connect with family, friends, and acquaintances. You are more popular, less stressed, happier, and more apt to have a sense of purpose.

Here is Dan Buettner describing and summarizing the attributes of people who do live longer, in his own words:

> *Maybe you've noticed that the world's longevity all-stars not only live longer, but they also tend to live better. They have strong connections with their family and friends. They're active. They wake up in the morning knowing that they have a purpose, and the world, in turn, reacts to them in a way that propels them along. An overwhelming majority of them still enjoy life. And there's not a grump in the bunch.* (Dan Buettner 2012)

As you can see, there is an essence in longevity planning that is intuitive and brings together many of the common threads previously covered in this book. If you make good daily choices, you have a greater probability of maintaining a healthier life and perhaps a longer one.

Having a sense of purpose (the why or what to live for) drives your energy and decisions into a focused direction. This elevates your happiness levels and ultimately enhances your legacy for who you are, whose lives you have touched, and what you have accomplished. Next we will cover the mindset of what it takes to age gracefully.

# Longevity Ideas

*If I'm not hungry and I'm busy, I am quite happy to skip a meal. It's informal intermittent fasting. I feel strongly that this is one of the strongest areas of longevity research.* (David Sinclair)

*Get around people who have something of value to share with you. Their impact will continue to have a significant effect on your life long after they have departed.* (Jim Rohn)

*It is better to have a meaningful life and make a difference than to merely have a long life.* (Bryant McGill)

*It's paradoxical that the idea of having a long life appeals to everyone but the idea of getting old doesn't appeal to anyone.* (Andy Rooney)

*The key to longevity is to interact with other people.* (Carl Reiner)

*What a man does for himself dies with him. What a man does for his community lives long after he's gone.* (Theodore Roosevelt)

*I'm most proud of the longevity of my marriage, my kids, and my grandchildren. If you don't have that, you really don't have very much.* (Bob Newhart)

*To continue to work, to continue to love what you do, is certainly a contributing element to one's longevity and health.* (John Williams)

*A sense of humor has been linked with longevity. It is a possibility that the mental attitude reflected in a lively sense of humor is an important factor predisposing some people toward long life.* (Raymond Moody)

*Living a long life, the conventional wisdom at the time said, depended to a great extent on who we were—that is, our genes. It depended on the decisions we made—on what we chose to eat, and how much we chose to exercise, and how effectively we were treated by the medical system. No one was used to thinking about health in terms of community.* (Malcolm Gladwell)

# CHAPTER 21

# Age Gracefully

*Don't complain about growing old—many, many people do not have that privilege.* (Earl Warren)

Life is short. We are all aging every minute of every day. Do not be afraid of growing older. Instead embrace it and don't waste a moment. Seize each day. Be disciplined and take charge of your health and of your life. Be optimistic. When you are, life is more fulfilling and pleasant. Stay in control of your physical, spiritual, and mental health. It requires a greater diligent effort, but it is well worth it because, when you do, you will greatly increase the probability of aging gracefully.

The first half of your life is about acquiring knowledge and focusing on family, school, and work. The second half of your life should be focused on purpose, health, and legacy. It is up to you to figure out how you choose to live and achieve it.

Here is Ilchi Lee on aging:

*Many studies have demonstrated the association between life extension and lifestyle, as those who have chosen unhealthy lives—drinking, smoking, being under too much stress—will have their life expectancies reduced by their choices. Those who have chosen healthy lives—developing good habits, exercising, and thinking positively—will have their life expectancies extended by their choices.* (Lee 2017)

You age gracefully when you apply wisdom in making lifestyle decisions. Sometimes it takes a little longer to acquire the proper perspectives on what really matters and what really is important. For those who seek nothing but pleasure in their teenage or early adult life, many of them fall behind as they age. That is because they sometimes take life for granted as they believe that life is too simple and easy. However, there is a long-term cost. There are skills not acquired, experiences not lived, habits not formed, and lessons not learned. It is like the Aesop Fable *The Tortoise and the Hare*, where the hare starts the race faster but eventually burns himself out and loses to the tortoise, who is slow but steady.

Live life to the fullest because life has an undeterminable expiration date. You also do not know when your health will begin to decline and are forced to slow down. Take advantage of your opportunities today and every day. Live with purpose and you will always be young at heart.

Think about this. Even if you were able to achieve mortality and live forever, would you be as motivated to find purpose and meaning? Wouldn't every day become routine and even boring knowing that time is endless, and deadlines are inconsequential? It is because life is uncertain that goals and tasks need to be planned out with timelines. This makes life interesting and prompts you to have a greater sense of urgency.

Here are some beautiful and scholarly thoughts about aging from Morrie Schwartz in *Tuesdays with Morrie*:

> *... I embrace aging ... It's very simple. As you grow, you learn more. If you stopped at twenty-two, you'd always be as ignorant as you were at twenty-two. Aging is not just decay, you know. It's growth ... The truth is, part of me is every age. I'm a three-year-old, I'm a five-year-old. I'm a thirty-seven-year-old, I'm a fifty-year-old. I've been through all of them, and I know what it's like. I delight in being a child when it's appropriate to be a child. I delight in being a wise old man when it's appropriate to be a wise old man. Think of all I can be! I am every age, up to my own.* (Albom 1997)

Be proactive about your health. Be curious and aggressive in managing your health literacy. Stay active and maintain good relationships and social networks. Be flexible and adjust your behaviors to what is appropriate for your age.

Finally, here is an excerpt from Andrew Weil as he highlights a twelve-point program for healthy aging. These are intuitive and have been mainly covered. Here are the final three points of the twelve that provide sound and fresh practical advice:

10. *Think about and try to discover for yourself the benefits of aging.*
11. *Do not deny the reality of aging or put energy into stopping it. Use the experience of aging as a stimulus for spiritual awakening and growth.*

12. *Keep an ongoing record of the lessons you learn, the wisdom you gain, and the values you hold. At critical points in your life, read this over, add to it, revise it, and share it with people you care about."* (Weil 2005)

# Ageless Advice

*He who is of a calm and happy nature will hardly feel the pressure of age, but to him who is of an opposite disposition, youth and age are equally a burden.* (Plato)

*Those who love deeply never grow old; they may die of old age, but they die young.* (Benjamin Franklin)

*Anyone who keeps the ability to see beauty never grows old.* (Franz Kafka)

*To keep the heart unwrinkled, to be hopeful, kindly, cheerful, reverent—that is to triumph over old age.* (Thomas Bailey Aldrich)

*As for old age, embrace and love it. It abounds with pleasure if you know how to use it. The gradually declining years are among the sweetest in a man's life, and I maintain that, even when they have reached the extreme limit, they have their pleasure still.* (Seneca)

*Do not grow old no matter how long you live. Never cease to stand like curious children before the great mystery into which we were born.* (Albert Einstein)

*The great thing about getting older is that you don't lose all the other ages you've been.* (Madeline L'Engle)

*You don't stop laughing when you grow old, you grow old when you stop laughing.* (George Bernard Shaw)

*I want to get old gracefully. I want to have good posture; I want to be healthy and be an example for my children.* (Sting)

*The longer I live, the more beautiful life becomes.*
(Frank Lloyd Wright)

*The secret of staying young is to live honestly, eat slowly, and lie about your age.* (Lucille Ball)

# PART 3

## Your Legacy
### (Planning for now, later, and future generations)

# CHAPTER 22

# What Everyone Wants

*If you're going to live, leave a legacy. Make a mark on this world that can't be erased.* (Maya Angelou)

As we age, there are a few common denominators as to what everyone seems to want. I'd like to discuss two of the biggest.

People want to be able to maintain some control over their lives and their standard of living. This includes tasks or pleasures that sometimes are taken for granted such as being able to work, drive, and travel and independently perform activities of daily living. Control is slowly taken away from many seniors primarily as a function of declining health. As these activities are slowly removed, their world becomes smaller. Everyone's goal is to hang on to these normal routines for as long as possible, so that some semblance of dignity and grace can be preserved. Please have compassion for those who are losing control because at some point that could happen to any of us.

The second item that everyone wants is to be remembered favorably and to leave behind a legacy of distinction. In order to have a legacy, we must create and plan the legacy we want to have.

That requires careful thought, consideration, and action. How do we want to be defined and remembered? What traits, characteristics, accomplishments, or lessons do we want to leave behind? Who have we helped and can these deeds be passed forward to the next generation?

Here are a few more areas that reasonable and civilized people want. While those with some wealth may have the capacity and resources to do more financially, this list is universal for everyone, regardless of wealth, upbringing, background, or demographics.

- To reach their full potential, which is to grow into the life we want to have.
- To create a legacy we can be proud of; one that is planned for and earned.
- To make a positive contribution to society, our community, and the world.
- To give back to those less fortunate. Being humble enough to remember that when we are having a bad day or going through a rough patch, there are always people who are handicapped, distressed, or have it much worse than we ever had on our worst day.

In other words, we want to be a good person and to have an impact in this world while alive so that when we are no longer physically here, we are remembered favorably by future generations. Optimally, we want to accomplish this while we have control over our lives and still possess our mental and physical abilities. I love this excerpt from Ilchi Lee. It captures the essence of the main points in this chapter:

*What people ultimately want isn't money, cool cars, expensive clothing, or lofty titles. It's not material values, like the attainment of wealth and social status. What they want is the feeling that they can live freely and independently, the feeling of loving and being loved, the feeling that their lives are precious and valuable, the feeling that they are contributing to something bigger than themselves. In short, people want, more than anything else, the inner satisfaction that comes from the realizations of their highest values. (Lee 2017)*

Of course there are many people who are obsessed with the opposite. They are pursuing financial independence, cool cars, second homes, climbing up the corporate ladder; they are living in the material world. We have all been there and may still be there. Their aspirations are one of accumulation. They are making ends meet, busy raising families, stuck in the rat race of the corporate world and the rules of engagement. Their lives are in the fast lanes and sometimes there is just no time to think, to plan ahead, to have balance, or reflect on their lives. They are in the moment, taking each day as it unwinds. That's okay. There is nothing wrong with that. Hopefully, there will be time for them one day to slow down to think about their purpose, health, and legacy. Many will gradually evolve and get to that stage where it strikes them as a more urgent priority. It may be an event that triggers it or just an epiphany when they wake up one day and ask themselves, "What am I doing with my life?" This is when they try to figure out what they want, which is what ultimately everyone wants.

Unfortunately, many will not care either because of their environment, their lack of will, negative emotions or attitudes, the people they associate with, or their lack of vision. It is my hope that more people, through books like this or through other influences, can be reached and motivated to live a more enriched life. Everyone has something to offer and live for. They just need to recognize that and to find their way. It is my opinion that subconsciously everyone wants the same things in their lives. Everyone may have a different approach to getting there, while sadly, others have not or may never recognize this in time.

## Words of Wants

*What you leave behind is not engraved in stone monuments, but what is woven in the lives of others.* (Pericles)

*All good men and women must take responsibility to create legacies that will take the next generation to a level we could only imagine.* (Jim Rohn)

*Live, laugh, leave a legacy.* (Stephen Covey)

*What you do is your history. What you set in motion is your legacy.* (Leonard Sweet)

*It's not enough to have lived. We should be determined to live for something.* (Winston Churchill)

# CHAPTER 23

# Traditional Estate vs. Legacy Planning

*Do something today that your future self will thank you for.*
(Author Unknown)

**Traditional Estate Planning:** According to Investopedia, estate planning involves determining how an individual's assets will be preserved, managed, and distributed after death or in the event they become incapacitated.

The key is that money and healthcare are the primary focuses in traditional estate planning. What happens to your things and how do you want your healthcare and estate taken care of in case you are no longer able to care for yourself or upon your death? How should assets be titled? Who are the beneficiaries on various assets? Who is going to receive what and when? Are living or irrevocable trusts needed? What about a power of attorney or durable power of attorney for healthcare or to manage assets in case of diminished capacity? What about living wills? Or special bequests? It gets more complicated the larger the estate becomes, and even more complex if there are business ownerships, collectibles, or real assets such as real estate, commodities, equipment, etc. Another objective in traditional estate planning is to preserve assets from taxes.

The planning revolves around the process of the transfer and distribution of assets. Wills and trusts are legal documents that provide instruction and guidance as to how the financial obligations will be handled. An inventory of assets is compiled and categorized. Guardians for minor children are named for those with young children. Executors and contingent executors are named to oversee the terms of the wills or trusts. Funeral arrangements are considered and often made in advance. Investment assets are managed with your intended goals, risk tolerance, and timeline. Primary and contingent beneficiaries are named in certain investment and insurance holdings. Charitable gifting strategies are planned and implemented at the appropriate time according to the plan itself.

Traditional estate planning is about dotting the i's and crossing the t's, devising a plan for disability, healthcare, death, taxes, money, and charitable inclinations. It includes how accounts and assets should be titled and content incorporated into the trust documents. When you do this type of planning and depending upon the complexity and size of the estate, it typically can be coordinated with a financial advisor, an estate planning attorney, a tax accountant, and sometimes other specialists or experts, when needed.

Traditional estate planning is technical and can be cumbersome. Some people have difficulty making important decisions or they procrastinate. Let's face it, while it is an important topic, it is also quite unpleasant because people do not want to voluntarily think about their mortality.

When it comes to determining the disposition of all your assets, ultimately everything will be sent to one or more of the following choices. Your wealth will go to either your loved ones or named beneficiaries, to the IRS, or to the charities of your choice. Estate planning is not an easy field to navigate through without sound professional help.

On a professional level, I have spent a lot of time in this space to plan or collaborate with experts in order to help clients for retirement and estate planning. Since state and federal regulations and tax laws are constantly changing, it is important to periodically review your estate plans with your advisors. Additionally, your goals may change over time and be outdated. There are a lot of strategies, tools, insurance, and investment products available to help manage risk and tax mitigation for any type of simple or complex situation. Mistakes can be both costly and harmful to all parties involved. Please be proactive so that there are no hidden surprises later.

**Legacy Planning:** While traditional estate planning deals primarily with healthcare, taxes, and financial assets, legacy planning focuses on incorporating your values, traditions, life stories, and important memories into a legacy. In other words, it reflects who you and your family are at your core. While it is not directly correlated to what traditional estate planning entails, in many ways, it is just as important. Almost without exception, advisors do not cover legacy planning because the area is more abstract and not as concrete as the traditional planning process. Legacy planning is an ongoing process and not a once-and-done proposition.

A traditional estate plan is about planning for the eventual processing of your estate. It is more or less transactional. Legacy planning is about being remembered kindly into future generations. It is less about numbers and tax laws and more about your essence, your soul, your accomplishments, your friendships, your connections, and the love you leave behind. Traditional estate planning is more about leaving a material monetary legacy while legacy planning is more about leaving a spiritual, nonmonetary, lasting message and memory.

Authors Perry Cochell and Rod Zeeb contrast the difference in their book *Beating the Midas Curse*:

> *Your personal legacy will be defined by generations by what you* valued, *not by the value of what you owned.* (Cochell and Zeeb 2014)

Legacy is also about the here and now. You are creating your legacy every day, with or without deliberate intent. Legacy is about choices you make and behavior that shapes your lifestyle. To be intentional about your legacy, you need to have purpose and meaning in your life.

While implementing both traditional estate and legacy planning is important for different reasons, the rest of this section will be dedicated to the various nuances of legacy planning. The focus will be primarily on nonmonetary areas with the partial exception of our discussion on charity and philanthropy.

# Principled Precepts

*The highest and best purpose of the estate planning process is, for me, to facilitate the effective transfer of an appropriate amount of financial assets to succeeding generations of family members in a way that will improve the life course.* (Charles Collier)

*A goal without a plan is just a wish.* (Author Unknown)

*By failing to prepare, you are preparing to fail.* (Benjamin Franklin)

*The greatest legacy one can pass on to one's children and grandchildren is not money or material things accumulated in one's life, but rather a legacy of character and faith.* (Billy Graham)

*My favorite things in life don't cost any money. It's really clear that the most precious resource we have is time.* (Steve Jobs)

*Please think about your legacy because you are writing it every day.* (Gary Vaynerchuk)

## CHAPTER 24

# Your Moral Autobiography

*Your story is the greatest legacy that you will leave to your
friends. It's the longest-lasting legacy you will leave to your heirs.*
(Steve Saint)

A moral biography is your life story. It is a part of the legacy you leave to your family and society. It is the story that outlives you when you are no longer alive. It is the part of you that lives on in the minds and hearts of others. It is the messages, values, stories, morals, and teachings by which you are remembered. It is the link that connects the past, present, and future.

A moral biography is essentially your final teaching. It is your opportunity to compile memories and combine them with meaning to motivate and lift others up. While you can share your traditions and values, try to fill your life with love, kindness, wisdom, faith, respect, and honor. That way you can lead by example. Be the hero of your own story, with the confidence that you led a life of significance and made a difference in this world. A moral biography is your legacy and represents symbolic immortality.

At the end of the day, real value is not about wealth. There are no dollar signs attached to it. Real wealth is what you have accomplished, who you have helped, the love you have left behind. It is about your heart, your soul, your integrity, your morality, and your character. It is about the quality relationships you had. While money can buy you things and status, it cannot buy you virtue and dignity. Money is a means to an end but not truly the end itself.

A moral biography can be written. You can write a personal mission statement, also known as an ethical will. This is a statement that reflects your values, thoughts, or philosophy of life. It is a legacy written to your children or loved ones that highlights and summarizes the legacy you want to leave and how you want to be remembered into the next generations. It can also pay homage to your ancestors from the past so that they are also remembered and never forgotten. Use pictures, videos, objects, diagrams, books, mementos, or other consequential items to supplement your story.

A moral biography can also be oral. Recreate past experiences and share stories and life lessons. All of you have had interesting and unique adventures. Recall warm, funny, and fond memories of ancestors, loved ones, and yourself. Share them with others over time. When you recall these memories, it binds people together. Some memories are bittersweet. The experience can be enriching, funny, moving, and entertaining, yet meaningful.

A moral biography could incorporate the hardships you suffered or endured throughout your life. What did you learn? How did you get here? What are some of your favorite recollections that your friends and loved ones do not know? What are you most proud of? What principles are most important? What wisdom can you pass on with the knowledge you acquired?

Of course, money and tangible wealth is important. I am not diminishing the value of traditional retirement or estate planning. What I am emphasizing is how much families cherish the life lessons, values, traditions, and stories that they can cling to and pass on to future generations. While the cost of creating a memory is negligible, the benefit is priceless. We should live to make wonderful and meaningful memories. It is these beautiful moments that we want to experience, remember, share, and leave behind.

Here are some profound thoughts from author Scott Fithian:

*The best decisions in life are made in view of one's ultimate end . . . There is something in the human body that wants to know that having been here has made a difference; it's part of our physical makeup . . . People need to connect with the stories and experiences of their past in order to gain clarity about the present.* (Fithian and Fithian 2007)

My interpretation of what Scott Fithian is saying is that you need to reflect on your past in order to connect with your present. This step is imperative to building your future legacy with intentionality. Ken Druck elaborates on this topic in his own way:

*The investment we make with our generosity, forgiveness, affection, patience, and humility may someday make us "people-rich" beyond our wildest dreams.* (Druck 2013)

At the end of the day, what do you want your moral biography to be? Are you making the nonmonetary investments that Ken Druck references above? What is your life story up to this point? How do you want to be remembered? Who else do you want to connect or reconnect with who has been important or impactful, to share life experiences and memories? Have you conveyed that message of purpose and meaning down to those you love? What do you imagine you might say to your loved ones at the end of your life? How you answer these questions and how you act on them over time will serve as the foundation for your legacy.

## Memorable Suggestions

*Everyone is necessarily the hero of his own life story.* (John Barth)

*Despite the natural belittling of oneself, the doubts, the insecurities, we have to wake up to the realization that we all write our own autobiography, we are the authors of our life story. Realizing that, write a good story with your life and make sure to write yourself as the protagonist. Be the hero of your journey.* (Yossi Ghinsberg)

*So yes I know how angry, or naïve, or self-destructive, or messed up, or even deluded I sound weaving my way through these life stories at times. But beautiful things. Graceful things. Hopeful things can sometimes appear in dark places.* (Lidia Yuknavitch)

*I'm writing an unauthorized autobiography.* (Steven Wright)

# CHAPTER 25

# Friends and Family

*Live so that when your children think of fairness, caring, and integrity, they think of you.* (H. Jackson Brown, Jr.)

Piggybacking from the last chapter, when you create and shape your legacy, there is no better audience than friends and family. While you can leave an indelible mark in your community and our society, you will most likely need others to join with you to guide and assist. People who know you, understand you, and are most familiar with you. These are the folks that you are generally closest to. Your legacy may be intertwined with theirs.

Never underestimate the importance of friends and true friendship. A real friend is someone you can talk to under any circumstances. You are there for each other without preconditions or asking for anything in return. In the course of a lifetime, friends tend to come in and out of your life. However, similar to having a loving pet, true friends are invaluable in forming wonderful memories and experiences. True friends become a part of your family and vice versa.

Your actual family is the group of individuals with whom you have the most history. You share direct lineal descent from generation to generation and so many amazing family stories that should be preserved. There are probably countless precious lessons and principles to learn from them. Think of all the history and how their lives were so different from yours. So you are the glue that binds everything together. You can take the best, funniest, or most pertinent parts of your past and pass that on to the next generation. Of course, any recipients should also have a desire and a willingness to embrace, record, and remember them.

The memories that you have of your parents, grandparents, other relatives, and ancestors can be quite compelling. That is because of the emotional and spiritual impact that they have on you. Their memories live through you, and at some point your memories will live on through your children, friends, and other family members. These recollections are more than just ordinary impressions. They have an emotional element that brings meaning. It is these special memories that you want to bottle up and pass down so that stories become legendary and never die. Sometimes legends just get bigger.

Family dynamics change over time. For example, as children grow older, there is a balancing act that takes place as family members, children in particular, need their individuality while still wanting to belong to their family. They want to have control of their own lives and still remain connected to the family and its heritage. Helping them bridge that gap allows you to keep that shared identity and perhaps a shared purpose.

However, there can be friction between the two, as author and philanthropic advisor Charles Collier points out:

*There is a tension between being an individual in a family and being a part of the whole. All families exhibit two strong emotional forces: one pushes us toward togetherness, while the other pulls us toward individuality ... The equilibrium of togetherness and individuality changes automatically and deliberately over time.* (Collier 2006)

Be aware of these changes and stay on top of them. Family members need independence while still maintaining the close family bond. Help them achieve both.

So what legacy do you want to leave to your family, friends, and society? Have you given it much thought, particularly if you are older? What about those of you who are younger reading this? Have you ever thought about not only your legacy but those of your parents, grandparents, or even great-grandparents? If you haven't, ask yourself: Why not? Should you? Should you carve out the time and rediscover your roots? Your bloodlines? Your genealogy? If there are some strong, angry emotions getting in the way of any of you, can you refocus and remember the fond memories or the good times you shared? Life is short and time moves quickly. Spend time with your loved ones while you can. Do not miss any opportunities to connect or make amends. That way, you will not have any regrets later.

Here is a poignant exercise about generational connection and legacy from Perry Cochell and Rod Zeeb:

*... every family has its own remarkable stories of trials and triumphs ... We leave you with this thought exercise ... Imagine that you are seated at one end of a very*

*long oak table in a great, vaulted hall. To your left extending so far out in the distance that you can only make out the dim outline of faces, sit your great-great-great-great grandparents. Next to them are their children, and then theirs, all of your ancestors up to and including your own parents, who sit on your immediate left ... This is your family. Gathered right here beside you, alive, brimming with stories of sacrifice and success, love and loss. A family woven together by a thread of values, stories, and experiences that intertwine across generations, and that will survive your passing and your children's, for generations to come.*

*Now, turn your gaze away from those who came before you, and look to your right. As you peer down the length of the table to a point far off in the distance ... imagine this: On your right sit your children. Next to them sit their children, and then your great-grandchildren, great-great grandchildren, and generations of their grandchildren. Dozens of generations yet to be born. Unlike the ancestors to your left who have lived their lives, each in different measure, and who now talk and laugh of times gone by, the heirs to the right are quiet. Each sits expectantly. Hope and anticipation fill their eyes.*

*Each holds an empty glass in his or her hand. Your task is to fill their glass to the brim. Fill it with memory and meaning, with values, that encourage, uplift, and motivate. Fill it with faith, honor, respect, and love. Fill it with your story.*

*When you leave a legacy that is built upon that kind of foundation, your descendants will not simply know your story. They will remember your name, what you stood for and believed in. They will honor your memory.* (Cochell and Zeeb 2014)

You are a link to the past and a bridge to the future. Both previous generations and ones not yet born are counting on you as you are the link in the chain between them. Share your most cherished family stories and memories so the chain can continue into future generations. Honor their memories. Additionally:

- Always remember where you came from and stay grounded.
- Embrace the opportunity to make great friendships and connect with those you are close to and love the most.
- Maximize the time you have. Leave a legacy that you are proud of and that others in future generations will look up to.
- Live your best life each day with purpose, meaning, and an eye toward the future.
- If you do, you won't be disappointed or regret it. Neither will the next generations that follow.

# Friendly Households

*In poverty and other misfortunes of life, true friends are a sure refuge. The young they keep out of mischief; to the old they are a comfort and aid in their weakness, and those in the prime of their life they incite to noble deeds.* (Aristotle)

*I cannot imagine a spiritual comfort deeper that dying with the knowledge that I had spent my brief time on this planet doing the best that I could to be present as myself to my family, my friends, my community, and my world.* (Parker Palmer)

*Families are like branches on a tree. We grow in different directions, yet our roots remain as one.* (Author Unknown)

*The only way to have a friend is to be one.*
(Ralph Waldo Emerson)

*Never forget where you came from and what your ancestors had to go through just for you.* (Author Unknown)

*There is so doubt that it is around the family and the home that all the greatest virtues, the most dominating virtues of human society, are created, strengthened and maintained.*
(Winston Churchill)

*Of all possessions a friend is the most precious.* (Herodotus)

*In family life, love is the oil that eases friction, the cement that binds closer together, and the music that brings harmony.* (Friedrich Nietzsche)

*Happiness is having a large, loving, caring, close-knit family in another city.* (George Burns)

# CHAPTER 26

# Tragedy and Death

*The life given us by nature is short, but the memory of*
*a life well spent is eternal.* (Cicero)

This certainly is never a pleasant topic, but an important one nevertheless that needs to be confronted and addressed. If you think about the history of the world using whatever starting point that suits you, we are alive for the equivalent time as a coffee break. In the scheme of things, it's not that long. Let's face it, time does fly, and life goes by quickly. Life is a roller coaster with many ups and downs, twists and turns. Sometimes you never know the direction to which it is heading. Tragedy and death are an inevitable part of the journey. As you can sometimes prepare for these events rationally, your emotional side may never be ready. That is stating the obvious.

Tragedy is something that you cannot plan around. It is something that you cannot dream your way out of, think your way out of, or buy your way out of. It just happens. How you react is the only thing that you can control. Don't let tragedy define you. Find the strength to move on.

You can give comfort and support to those who are suffering and grieving. While no one can necessarily provide answers as to why something has happened, we can provide strength and hope to those who need it. When someone dies, grieving has a timetable and a timetable all to itself. Some things just hurt for a long time and healing can be a lengthy process. Sometimes it never gets better; it just gets different. It takes patience and small steps to go forward. New or old feelings surface and need to be validated or reconciled. It takes determination and courage at times to heal.

Truly understanding, accepting, and embracing your own mortality can act as an added incentive to make a difference and lead a life of purpose and significance. After all, it is a race against time for all of us. Just like a game of musical chairs, we are here until the music stops and there is no place to sit.

Here is Viktor Frankl on that very subject.

> *The fact, and only the fact, that we are mortal, that our lives are finite, that our time is restricted and our possibilities are limited, this fact is what makes it meaningful to do something, to exploit a possibility and make it become a reality, to fulfill it, to use our time and occupy it. Death gives us a compulsion to do so. Therefore, death forms the background against which our act of being becomes a responsibility.* (Frankl 2020)

Ilchi Lee describes mortality this way.

> *Although we can't take anything we've obtained in the world with us when we die, we can take this one thing—our*

*souls. Your soul is the essence of your being, the only thing
you always have with you, transcending even death. Your
soul is the true self you are seeking.* (Lee 2017)

Knowing that life is limited, be conscious of your time. Have
a plan and make things happen. Have the fortitude to live the life
you want to live, one that fits your lifestyle, character, and budget.
Be disciplined but be flexible enough to adapt to what lies ahead. If
you believe that you have lived your life with purpose and significance, you will experience tranquility. You will eventually be able
to confront death with peace and comfort.

Harold Kushner addressed the fear of dying this way as he was
having a conversation with a clergyman friend of his who was
struggling with visiting a member of his congregation who was
hospitalized with an inoperable brain tumor:

*I think I understand why you do that. I suspect that you
see too much of yourself in him. Seeing him ill and dying
makes you think that a year from now, it could be you in
that situation, and you can't handle that. I would guess
that you are afraid of dying—it's nothing to be ashamed
of, lots of people are—and that is why seeing someone your
own age dying is so hard for you to deal with.*

*"How do you get over the fear of dying?" he asked me. I
told him that I was not ready to die, that I hoped to live for
many more years, but I was not afraid of dying because I
felt satisfied with what I had done with my life. I had the
sense that I had not wasted it, and that I had lived with*

*integrity, had done my best, and had an impact on people which would outlast me ... It is only when you are no longer afraid to die that you can say you are truly alive.*

*I believe that it is not dying that people are afraid of. Something else, something more unsettling and more tragic than dying frightens us. We are afraid of never having lived, of coming to the end of our days with the sense that we were never really alive, that we never figured out what life was for.* (Kushner 1986)

Then there is Ken Druck reflecting his own thoughts about the topic of mortality.

*There's no negotiability with death; someday we're all going to die. But since we don't get a final say about when that's going to happen, how are we supposed to live? Why not let go of at least some of the fear and embrace the unknown and unknowable elements of death? Cherish every moment we have? Hold our beliefs about what happens when we die as our "faith"?*

*With this approach to life, every day becomes sacred. Every relationship becomes a chance for a true connection and meeting between two people. What if we begin to really cherish the people in our lives and the privilege of being with them every day? And treat ourselves in the same way, championing our health and doing things that will give us a better chance at a longer, happier life?* (Druck 2013)

Here are guidelines to consider because all of us will be confronted with the challenges and sadness of tragedy and death. Hopefully, this will give you conviction for living the best life you can for as long as you can, with the awareness that everything in life can abruptly change at any time. That is why you must take full advantage of the opportunities and blessings you have when there is no distress surrounding you.

- Always be grateful that you are alive.
- Live in the present and stay true to yourself.
- Do what you can to stay healthy for as long as you can.
- Never take anything for granted as things can change abruptly.
- Stay calm and think clearly when tragedy strikes.
- Reach out and comfort others who are suffering from their tragedies.
- Live your own life and not the life of someone else.
- Follow your passions, heart, and intuition. Live your life with grace and dignity.
- Develop a life purpose with an eye toward your legacy.
- Since life is a mystery that is constantly unfolding, and has an uncertain end date, try to love every moment of every day!

Finally, I would like to conclude this chapter with a tribute to all those who have passed on. This is something I wrote in 2017 at the one-year ceremony of my mother's passing. It was when my family met at her gravesite for the unveiling of her tombstone. It was originally written in honor of my mother and father, who were finally together in perpetuity. My father had passed away in 2012. In looking around the cemetery, I realized that the message was generic enough to honor not only my other relatives who were buried there but for anyone and everyone, regardless of the location, who was deceased and should be remembered and revered. It was composed as a cross between a poem, prayer, and psalm. I also admit that I wrote this for myself, with the theme imbedded deep into my heart. The desire is for you to find it meaningful and that it becomes more of a universal accolade, an anthem of sorts, for all our ancestors, friends, colleagues, and role models. Bless them all!

## WE WILL ALWAYS REMEMBER

We are here to honor, praise, and celebrate you;
Your spirit is with us; it emanates through.

Great stories we share; images we deploy,
Recalling our past, rekindling our joy.

*Your memories remain with us; our love lasts forever;*
*You will never be forgotten; we will always remember.*

Your life was a gift, a treasure chest of love;
You touched the lives of many; you were so beloved.

Your legacy grows as does all our ancestors too;
You are all a part of us; we are all a part of you.

*Looking back in time our lives remain tethered;*
*Your presence is everywhere; we will always remember.*

We are reminded of your kindness; we still hear your voice;
You warm up our hearts; you inspire us to rejoice.

We know life is complex with its many ups and downs,
With countless emotions, such as happiness, sadness, smiles,
and frowns.

*No matter what time of year from January to December,*
*You are never far from our thoughts; we will always remember.*

We get busy and lost, absorbed in our daily routines,
But you are nearby when we call for you; we all have the means.

When we think of you, it lifts up our mood
and puts a smile on our face,
Then our stress is diminished; our sorrows erased.

*We have eternally bonded, our lives woven together;*
*We will never forget you; we will always remember.*

We are humbled to have known you; our souls been advanced;
Your generosity was noticed; our lives so enhanced.

To future generations the lessons you taught us
must always be retained,
So let us share our fond memories, then your love and
compassion will forever be maintained.

*Your life was a gift to us, something we all cherish together;*
*Thank you for everything; we will always remember.*

# Solemn Observations

*You live as long as someone speaks your name.*
(American Indian saying)

*Tragedy is a tool for the living to gain wisdom, and a guide by which to live by.* (Robert Kennedy)

*Even death is not to be feared by one who has lived wisely.* (Buddha)

*It is not death that a man should fear, but he should fear never beginning to live.* (Marcus Aurelius)

*Immortality is to live your life doing good things and leaving your mark behind.* (Brandon Lee)

*Life is pleasant. Death is peaceful. It's the transition that's troublesome.* (Isaac Asimov)

*When good men die, their goodness does not perish but lives though they are gone. As of the bad, all that was theirs dies and is buried with them.* (Euripides)

*The greatest dignity to be found in death is the dignity of the life that preceded it. Hope resides in the meaning of what our lives have been.* (Sherwin Nuland)

*Remembering that I'll be dead soon is the most important tool I've ever encountered to help me make choices in life. Because almost everything—all external expectations, all pride, all fear of embarrassment or failure—these things just fall away in the face of death, leaving only what is truly important.* (Steve Jobs)

Since this is such a heavy topic, here are a few comedic one-liners just to lighten it up a bit. The bottom line is that there is humor in everything if you look for it.

*I don't want to achieve immortality through my work. I want to achieve it by not dying.* (Woody Allen)

*My fake plants died because I did not pretend to water them.* (Mitch Hedberg)

*If you die in an elevator, be sure to push the up button.* (Sam Levinson)

*I am not afraid of death; I just don't want to be there when it happens.* (Woody Allen)

*I can't afford to die; I'd lose too much money.* (George Burns)

*I intend to live forever or die trying.* (Groucho Marx)

# CHAPTER 27

# Knowledge and Wisdom

*I am the wisest man alive for I know one thing
and that is I know nothing.* (Plato)

Both knowledge and wisdom can play an important part in pursuing a meaningful legacy, and a sense of purpose. At its core, knowledge refers to learning through education while wisdom is knowing when and how to apply the knowledge that you have obtained. You spend much of your life learning and accumulating knowledge. You also acquire knowledge through skills and life experiences over time. It is always prudent practice to continue striving to learn, to be curious, to sharpen your skills, and to have a quest to amass more knowledge, no matter what your age is. That enables you to continue to grow intellectually, to be interesting and relevant.

Wisdom is using your knowledge to make a positive impact and help others. Wisdom is knowing yourself, your limitations, and your strengths. It is the ability to think clearly and adjust your decision-making when needed. It is having a heightened intuition and knowing how and when to rely on it. Wisdom is using the knowledge you gain over your lifespan and steering it into the direction of purpose and legacy. You need wisdom in order to thrive.

There is sometimes a fine line between knowledge and wisdom. For example, a teacher needs to know when to be gentle or when to be candid when dealing with a struggling student and how best to motivate and help them. It is knowing what to say, how to say it, and when to say it. We are a rules-based society that dictates our behavior, but there are times when rules can be flexible or bent. A good doctor will be honest and kind to a patient when delivering bad news but will try to balance that with hope. Sometimes a diagnosis or treatment could be problematic, and the doctor must decide whether it is better to be blunt, kind, or hopeful when talking to the patient. This requires experience, compassion, maturity, and wisdom. Business owners also need to be flexible and make suitable adjustments as business conditions dictate. Examples could include making good decisions on strategic planning, acquisitions, marketing, and personnel decisions, just to name a few. When you effectively use your knowledge to make wise decisions, you have the power to positively change lives.

Aristotle described this as "practical wisdom" or what he called phronesis. That is the practice of using sound judgment and knowing what to do in any extraordinary situation. Practical wisdom requires empathy, flexibility, adaptability, creativity, integrity, and compassion in dealing with other people. It requires deeper nuanced thinking and thought process. It cannot be taught in a textbook or learned as a general skill. Wisdom can be acquired partly through experience. It can be accelerated when novices learn from mentors who coach them properly. Eventually, novices learn to think independently and become the new mentors. It is not always related to age as anyone at any age could apply practical wisdom. Likewise, not everyone becomes wiser as they get older.

Here are some superb excerpts about the subject matter from authors Barry Schwartz and Kenneth Sharp in their book *Practical Wisdom*. The discussion revolves around Aristotle and his critical thoughts revolving around wisdom.

> *He thought that our fundamental social practices constantly demanded choices—like when to be loyal to a friend, or how to be fair, or how to confront risk, or when and how to be angry—and that making the right choices demanded wisdom... The wisdom... to act rightly was distinctly practical, not theoretical. It depended on our ability to perceive the situation, to have the appropriate feelings or desires about it, to deliberate about what was appropriate in those circumstances, and to act.* (Schwartz and Sharpe 2011)

> *The wiser we are in what we do, the happier we are... Aristotle understood this when he argued for the importance of practical wisdom. The purpose of life, he insisted, was human flourishing—what we translate as happiness. But you couldn't flourish unless you had the wit and skill to make every day ethical choices. Practical wisdom was what provided that skill and wit. With practical wisdom, we flourish; without it, we languish.* (Schwartz and Sharpe 2011)

So let's sum this up like this. You can have knowledge about many topics but still lack wisdom. There is also a correlation between normal common sense and wisdom in that both can sometimes be applied independently of specific training or knowledge acquired. Another way of saying it is that one can be book smart but not street smart. Recognize that learning leads to knowledge. New experiences and skills can also result in increased knowledge. Wisdom comes when you apply everything you have learned to grow, succeed, and help others. Wisdom is learning and adapting from your mistakes. It also takes courage, as well as wisdom, to apply knowledge and do the right things for the right reasons, regardless of external pressures. When you are attempting to make the wisest choices possible, slow yourself down, tune out the noises surrounding you, be rational, mindful, deliberate, and evaluate your choices from multiple angles. See the big picture and take your emotions out of the equation.

Wisdom is virtuous. It gives you the know-how to do right by others and for yourself. Having the right balance of knowledge and wisdom may help define who you are, what you stand for, and what you do. Wisdom needs to be practical and in the moment because the choices you make can be complex. While knowledge will help you in many aspects of your life, it is your wisdom that will bring integrity, underscoring your allegiance to ethical principles, honesty, and righteous moral behavior. When you have achieved this level of wisdom, an honorable reputation will follow that will continue to add to your legacy. It is wisdom that ultimately people will remember you for. The distinction between knowledge and wisdom is important and should always be regarded. It is never too late to learn, and it is never too late to become wiser and make judicious choices.

I thought it would be appropriate to finish this chapter by highlighting the elegant and splendid first verse of "The Serenity Prayer." It was attributed to Reinhold Niebuhr (1892-1971). This famous prayer is beautiful and teaches all of us about how to live our daily lives while applying "practical wisdom."

*God grant me the serenity*
*To accept the things I cannot change;*
*Courage to change the things I can;*
*And wisdom to know the difference.*

# Astute Writings

*The greatest thing in life is experience. Even mistakes have value.* (Henry Ford)

*Knowledge can be communicated, but not wisdom. One can find it, live it, be fortified by it, do wonders through it, but one cannot communicate and teach it.* (Hermann Hesse)

*Wisdom is not a product of schooling but of the lifelong attempt to acquire it.* (Albert Einstein)

*Knowledge is a process of piling up facts; wisdom lies in their simplification.* (Martin Luther King, Jr.)

*The greatest enemy of knowledge is not ignorance; it is the illusion of knowledge.* (Stephen Hawking)

*By three methods we may learn wisdom: First, by reflection, which is noblest; Second, by imitation, which is easiest; and Third by experience, which is the bitterest.* (Confucius)

*Wisdom is the right use of knowledge. To know is not to be wise. Many men know a great deal and are all the greater fools for it. There is no fool so great a fool as a knowing fool. But to know how to use knowledge is to have wisdom.* (Charles Spurgeon)

*A good listener is not only popular everywhere, but after a while he gets to know something.* (Wilson Mizner)

# CHAPTER 28

# Love

*The best and most beautiful things in the world cannot be seen or even touched—they must be felt with the heart.* (Hellen Keller)

When you look up the definition of the word *love*, the following are just a few of the adjectives that come up: affection, adoration, devotion, worship, passion, intimacy, commitment, care, closeness, protectiveness, attraction, trust, lust, and friendship. This chapter will focus on how love relates to your legacy.

Love is our greatest desire. You want to love and be loved. It is satisfying to have loving relationships in your life. You need others to share life's journey, those you trust and love. It is gratifying to give love and make a difference in someone else's life. As Viktor Frankl stated, acts of love and care also provide a sense of purpose for those who need comfort in times of their greatest need. Love does not protect us from tragedy, death, and loss but it makes everything more bearable. You are better equipped to survive and overcome loss because of the healing power of love and intimacy that surrounds it. When you have loving relationships, you are never lonely and you are truly not alone. There is comfort in that.

Hate is the opposite emotion of love. When you believe you are a victim, it trickles down to your subconscious mind. The more your belief of victimhood grows, the more intense your hatred builds. Hate crowds out your capacity for enjoyment, joy, love, and happiness. It also takes away from your peace of mind, any semblance of serenity, and a part of your soul. When you are down and out, one good remedy to lessen your pain is to reach out and help someone else. By helping someone else, it makes you feel better about yourself, as it is an act of love and kindness. When you are depressed and not in a good place in life, remind yourself that sometimes it is necessary that you live for others because they do love and need you. Your loved ones are significantly better off with you in their lives than without you.

When you have a strong relationship, you can open up and share more. That is what intimacy is about. Here is social scientist and author Arthur Brooks diving further into this topic.

*When you are honest and humble about your weaknesses, you will be more comfortable in your own skin. When you use your weaknesses to connect with others, love in your life will grow ... To share your weakness without caring what others think is a kind of superpower.* (Brooks 2022)

Here are some eloquent, deep, and inspiring thoughts about love from Morrie Schwartz as he was approaching the end of his life:

*And love is how you stay alive, even after you are gone.* (Albom 1997)

*As long as we can love each other, and remember the feeling of love we had, we can die without ever really going away. All the love you created is still there. All the memories are still there. You live on—in the hearts of everyone you have touched and nurtured while you were here . . . Death ends a life, not a relationship.* (Albom 1997)

While all of this is true about love and death, there is still a bridge to cross. After the loss of a dear loved one, how do survivors overcome their raw, intense emotions and move on? How do they get to that point where loving warm memories kick in and the true enduring legacy of their loved ones can begin? While the magnitude and duration of healing differ from person to person, authors Elisabeth Kübler-Ross and David Kessler elegantly address the importance and cycle of grieving:

*. . . grief is the healing process of the heart, soul, and mind; it is the path that returns us to wholeness . . . You will not "get over" the loss of a loved one; you will learn to deal with it. You will heal, and you will rebuild yourself around the loss you have suffered . . . With the power of grief comes much of the fruits of our grief and grieving . . . It completes an intense cycle of emotional upheaval. It doesn't mean we forget; it doesn't mean we are not revisited by the pain of loss. It does mean we have experienced life to its fullest, complete with the cycle of birth and death. We have survived loss. We are allowing the power of grief and grieving to help us to heal and to live with the one we lost.*

*That is the Grace of Grief. That is the Miracle of Grief.*
*That is the Gift of Grief.* (Kübler-Ross & Kessler 2005)

True love can be applied to loving pets. They bring the purest form of love; that being unconditional love. A good pet becomes an integral part of your life. They reduce stress and bring joy and are with you when you need a friend. They can provide you with a source of strength and companionship. They have unique personalities that can sometimes make you laugh when they are silly. The downside to owning a pet is their shorter lifespan. When you lose a pet, it's painful since they are a part of your family.

I am reminded of the famous line penned by Alfred Lord Tennyson. "It is better to have loved and lost than never to have loved at all." So true. You are better off having had the experience of being together with the time you had. (Of course, this also applies to human relationships.) The pleasure and bliss derived from their love far exceed the sorrow of their loss. Remember that sorrow is fleeting and these feelings are soon replaced by priceless memories of warmth and happiness. Loving pets teach you how to be compassionate; they make you a kinder, gentler person. They become a part of who you are and who you become. By interpolation, they become a part of your core being, and thus, a part of your legacy.

Love is beautiful while you're alive and does not disappear after your death, if you indeed live a life full of love. There are many ways to express and give love. Find what works best for you. Just know that the rewards of living a loving and caring life, one of integrity and humbleness, will continue on for the rest of your life and beyond. That is a meaningful and wonderful legacy to leave to your loved ones, your community, and the world. After all, the purest form of love has no boundaries and is eternal.

## Loving Lessons

*Love is like infinity. You can't have more or less infinity, and you can't compare two things to see if they're "equally infinite." Infinity just is, and that's the way I think love is too.* (Fred Rogers)

*Love has no age, no limit, and no death.* (John Galsworthy)

*Love is friendship that has caught fire. It is quiet understanding, mutual confidence, sharing and forgiving. It is loyalty through good and bad times. It settles for less than perfection and makes allowance for human weaknesses.* (Ann Landers)

*I don't think of all the misery, but of all the beauty that still remains.* (Anne Frank)

*Be in love with your life. Every minute of it.* (Jack Kerouac)

*Time is too slow for those who wait, too swift for those who fear, too long for those who grieve, too short for those who rejoice, but for those who love, time is eternity.* (Henry Van Dyke)

*I have found that if you love life, life will love you back.* (Arthur Rubinstein)

*What we have once enjoyed deeply we can never lose. All that we love deeply becomes a part of us.* (Hellen Keller)

*Money is not the most important thing in the world. Love is. Fortunately, I love money.* (Jackie Mason)

# CHAPTER 29

# Being Charitable vs. Philanthropic

*The great use of life is to spend it for something that will outlast it.*
(William James)

Andrew Carnegie was a steel tycoon, had a reputation for being shrewd and ruthless, and became one of the wealthiest businessmen in America in the late nineteenth century. Later in life his priorities changed as he became a leading philanthropist and dedicated the rest of his life to many philanthropic causes for social and educational advancement. By the time he died in 1919, he had given away around 90 percent of his enormous wealth. His actions inspired many others to find their own ways to give back to society.

There are many ways you can give back to the community or perhaps to larger endowments. People tend to give more to causes that they are more passionate about or to issues that they are trying to make an impact on to promote real change. Gifts are not always about money as the gift of time and leadership may sometimes be more valuable than money donated.

Giving back makes you feel proud because you are doing something beneficial for others. It is also a way of giving back to society and paying it forward for everything that has gone well in your life. Giving from your heart is the purest form of altruism and can be another method of defining your sense of purpose. In true legacy planning, community, family, and your own personal legacy values are melded together. It is being purposeful about your goals and what you are looking to accomplish. When done to your satisfaction, it can be empowering to know that you have done your best to make the world a better place. True and intentional legacy planning is an ongoing process and not a one-time event. It is best accomplished when you incorporate your values and match them with your legacy intentions.

There are many overlapping principles for being charitable and philanthropic as they are both about giving of yourself or your wealth. There are some differences in terms of impact and style. Both can involve volunteering your time, skills, leadership abilities, and money/wealth.

**Being Charitable:** This can be giving to others out of kindness, being impulsive, or being responsive, such as when you give something to someone because you are moved, or you feel obligated. Examples would include giving to disaster relief, or to someone you see who is cold or hungry, buying cookies for Girl or Boy Scouts, or making donations to volunteers who are soliciting for various causes.

There are other occasions that you give when asked. It can be to organizations that you recognize. Some of these may be annual or traditional gifts and are more responsive forms of charitable giving. These are also more like checkbook giving, where you give money but are not emotionally attached to the charity or the cause.

Tithing is another form of giving back to your community, parish, church, etc.

Volunteering can mean working to raise money for a worthy cause or collecting clothes for people in need. It can be to rally the community for shared values such as for a religious affiliation or a nonprofit organization. It can also be using your talents to create something to help the poor or patients in nursing homes.

**Being Philanthropic:** If you are a philanthropist, it is typically more about giving from your heart with issues or causes you identify with and are important to you. Philanthropy donors tend to give larger monetary amounts and carefully plan how much to give to nonprofits and what to leave to family. Philanthropy, if done properly, allows you to perceive a sense of immortality through a detailed and authentic plan of giving and making a difference. It can be a way of expressing your core values while providing the virtue of care. It connects money to meaning.

Philanthropy can be strategic with an objective to achieve a desired result. It can also be aligned with investments constructed for impact and for the greater good. Examples of these would include improving education for a certain topic, providing food and shelter to people in need, helping reduce crime, or helping to cure a specific disease.

Another approach is to be a social entrepreneur by creating a business start-up that is formed with impact or activism in mind. These types of businesses can either be a nonprofit or a for-profit enterprise. Sometimes being an expert who investigates causes, drafts white papers, or gives out grants can be the right path for you, if there is a match of skills and desire.

Being philanthropic requires detailed planning, which begins with aligning your deepest levels of values to what your call to action is. It coordinates your moral capacity with your financial capacity. After careful consideration of why you are wanting to give, then you can start to plan how to accomplish your vision and your goals. There are many tools, techniques, and tax laws that are part of the planning process and can provide some ancillary benefits to you and your family. The larger the gifts, the more a team of advisors is needed to help you sort out the details, strategies, and complexities.

Philanthropy is personal. Philanthropists are generally accountable to no one but themselves. Your plan can include giving while you are alive and/or at death for impact. In many cases, it can incorporate family members, which allows the philanthropy to be managed and passed on from one generation to the next. To enhance the probability of success, it is important that family members have shared values, purpose, vision, and identity. Family foundations are frequently created for multi-generational timelines.

**Other considerations:** There are those among you who start out as a "checkbook" charitable giver and eventually transition into being philanthropic with greater intention. Keep in mind that your legacy is a combination of your life's work, life lessons, traditions, values, memories, and character, as well as your charitable and philanthropic life's work. When you give back to your community, your community continues to live on through you and because of you. In essence the world becomes a better place because of your well-thought-out deliberate planning. That also provides purpose and is a euphoric feeling!

As previously stated in our review of traditional estate planning, you have only three choices where your wealth will go to upon your death. It is either going to your family/ loved ones, taxes, or charity. With careful planning, you can choose how you want to allocate your wealth. Additionally, you have three areas that you are capable of donating or giving to those you wish to help: your time, talent, or treasures/wealth.

Here are some important preliminary questions to ask yourself before you start this process:

- How much do you need to live on while you're alive or to achieve and to maintain financial independence?
- How much do you want to leave your loved ones?
- How much would you like to leave to charities or causes you care about?
- Besides you and your family, is (are) there any issue(s) or causes(s) in the world that you feel passionate about enough to drive you to make a positive impact?
- What do you feel is the most important lesson or characteristic you can pass on to your heirs when it comes to your thoughts or philosophy about charitable giving or philanthropy?
- How do you want to be remembered in future generations when it comes to giving back?

# Charitable Chatter

*We make a living by what we get, but we make a life by what we give.* (Winston Churchill)

*No one has ever become poor by giving.* (Anne Frank)

*Every charitable act is a stepping stone towards heaven.* (Henry Ward Beecher)

*The best way to find yourself is to lose yourself in the service of others.* (Mahatma Gandhi)

*The alignment of one's passion to one's giving is often elusive, but worth the search.* (Peter Karoff)

*Life is a gift, and it offers us the privilege, opportunity, and responsibility to give something back by becoming more.* (Tony Robbins)

*Philanthropy is almost the only virtue which is sufficiently appreciated by mankind.* (Henry David Thoreau)

*If I win the lottery, I'm giving all my money to Charity. If she's not dancing that night, I'm giving it all to Destiny.* (Author Unknown)

## CHAPTER 30

# What Matters Most

*Life is short. Focus on what really matters most; you should change your priorities over time.* (Roy T. Bennett)

Let us take a few brief moments to summarize the key points in the first three sections of this book before we move on:

- First and foremost, find purpose in your life.
- Stay focused and disciplined in managing your health.
- Be mindful of your legacy both for today and how it impacts future generations.

While there are always going to be concerns and issues that are out of your control, focus on what you can control and try to stay positive. Maintaining good health requires discipline and calculated daily decisions as to eating, exercising, sleeping, and managing your stress levels. When you take care of your health, it is easier, although not a prerequisite, to enjoy and take advantage of everything that is wonderful about life. Always remember to laugh a lot and enjoy the ride along the way. Commit to a lifelong process of learning and keeping your brain active.

Generally, the first half of your life is dedicated to growing up into adulthood, making certain life choices such as education, careers, and family matters. For many, it is about raising children, buying a home, traveling, and accumulating wealth. Life is complicated, moving fast, and there is not always a lot of free time to think clearly since there are many moving parts in your life. As your family grows up and (or if) life starts to slow down, there is another aspect or phase that many of you contemplate sometimes, even subconsciously at first. The topic that puzzles you is: What can you do to live a life of significance? What can you do that will bring purpose into your life? What can you do that will make you wake up every morning and provide you with a sense of urgency, excitement, or direction? What is your ultimate calling? What can you do that will make your life one of distinction? If you are unsure of what your purpose is, continue to search for it and don't be discouraged. Sometimes we find purpose and sometimes purpose finds us. Finding purpose brings overall greater stability.

Ultimately what matters most is to maintain control of your life as long as you can, to live a life of significance, and to leave behind a meaningful legacy. As previously stated, there are both monetary and nonmonetary methods to accomplish that. In looking back at your life, extract meaning and the lessons learned and, in doing so, pass some wisdom on to the next generation.

It is easy to get sidetracked with distractions and everyday drama. That can be okay but only for so long. When the distractions become too much, be in the moment. Remind yourself about what really is important and get back to what matters most.

Love and friendship matter since we are generally social creatures and relationship satisfaction brings a greater degree of happiness and inner peace. It may be argued that staying in love is even more important than falling in love.

Creating efficiency and a routine in your lifestyle leads to a better rhythm and harmony. Being able to see the big picture enables you to dedicate your time to developing your wholeness as a person. This includes your body, mind, heart, and soul, and aligning them to live your best life, with purpose, while building your legacy.

I want to end this chapter with some inciteful, poignant, and astute comments from Scott Fithian about not only purpose and legacy, but really about what matters most:

> *Legacy is about the here and now. It is about behavior, about how you live in this world rather than how you leave it. To be intentional about your legacy, you must know your purpose ... We are creating our legacies every second of every day. With or without intent, it's being formed—reputation, relationship, experiences, stories. Every word we speak and every decision we make. Every day we skirt around this reality is another day lost in the opportunity to shape it with intent ...*

> *Legacy is heritage and heritage is tradition. Traditions are actions captured. Legacy is the most important tool any human possesses. The world will go on forever after we're gone. How will each of us positively impact its trajectory? That is legacy.*

*...focus on life first, wealth second. Wealth is a topic, not a tradition. In the final hours, human connection is all that matters. That is legacy.* (Fithian and Fithian 2017)

# Matters of Reflection

*Don't be pushed by your problems. Be led by your dreams.*
(Ralph Waldo Emerson)

*The aim of life is self-development. To realize one's nature perfectly—that is what each of us is here for.* (Oscar Wilde)

*What matters most is how we respond to what we experience in life.* (Stephen Covey)

*If you ask yourself, "What's important now?" then you won't waste time on the trivia.* (Lou Holtz)

*Let us reflect on what is truly of value in life, what gives meaning to our lives, and set our priorities on the basis of that.* (Dalai Lama)

*Someone asked me, if I were stranded on a desert island what book would I bring...* How to Build a Boat. (Steven Wright)

# PART 4

## Further Insights for a Better Life
### (Finding balance and harmony)

# CHAPTER 31

# Life Is Complicated, Unfair, Yet Totally Fair

*Sometimes life is going to hit you in the head with a brick. Don't lose faith.* (Steve Jobs)

**L**ife is complicated: You can be torn in many directions, juggling different tasks or responsibilities, some days more than others. Most of you can handle a certain level of complexity and uncertainty in your normal routine. However, when you throw in some additional curveballs that stretch your capacity—such as losing your job, being betrayed by a friend, dealing with difficult personalities or undesirable outcomes, being blamed for something you are innocent of, illness, or death—then everything can become too complicated, overwhelming, and stressful. It can seem that you cannot catch a break. How should you cope with genuine complexity, sorrow, or heartbreak? How do you endure unbearable physical or emotional pain? How do you go on when you know that something happened that is not just or not right?

**Life is unfair:** You may agree with this description since there are aspects of life that do not seem fair, particularly from the list mentioned in the previous paragraph. Do bad things just happen or happen for a reason? Is it random or is part of a bigger plan? Why do people die when they do and why do people suffer so much when others don't? What about the saying that you will live happily ever after? Is that just a false premise?

It is logical to assume that life is not going to be linear or predictable. Love and then loss may seem to appear randomly. Changes can happen abruptly. Your life can get ugly or messy during that period. There is no way to sugarcoat it. Life can be quite difficult or sad at times, even gut-wrenching. It can be quite humbling and emotional. You are powerless to stop the reality of it and even comprehend what is happening around you. It is beyond your ability to understand why something horrible takes place in your life. Life is a conundrum. The world doesn't always make sense, and there is not always a cause and effect for everything bad that happens. Exceptions are not made for nice people, and sometimes the hurt is so extremely painful that it will shake you to your very soul.

**Life is totally fair:** There is a flip side to what happens in life. You already know rationally, in your mind, that things seem to never go completely as planned. That's just part of the roller coaster of life. However, when reality sets in, and stuff happens, you are never completely prepared mentally. It is how you respond to these situations that matters. These can be defining moments that can build character and personal growth and strengthen your core values. While you understand that life isn't always fair, remember that life is also more than fair, if you have the right perspective. Life is a gift and there are so many aspects of your life that have gone right and to your benefit. Many days are good days, and these days have outnumbered the bad days by an enormous amount. You have much to be grateful for, even during personal hardships. Recognize that out of hopelessness can come hope, faith, courage, trust, intimacy, and gratitude.

Don't ignore your inner struggles but acknowledge them when things are really bad. Feel the outrage. Give yourself some space to go through the cycle of emotions. Go ahead and allow yourself to be sad, angry, scared, frightened, disappointed, or helpless. Let it out and let it all come to the surface. Do not mask your pain with drugs or alcohol; let it all out naturally. Let it flow through you completely. Take the appropriate amount of time that you need.

Then calm yourself down, breathe, and lower your emotional temperature. Taking a walk or exercising might help you cope with the angst, stress, and emotional pain. It might provide you with the vehicle you need to think, analyze, and evaluate. Reflect on what happened. Allow your rational side to take over again (Daniel Kahneman's System 2: thinking slow). Check your attitude. Decide what needs to be done or what your next action steps are. What can or should you do? Do you need assistance along the way, and to whom would you reach out? At some point, if your troubles are permanent, you need to adjust your behavior to recognize the new reality. Let your setbacks go emotionally and move on.

Life is precious and there are many wonderful moments. Savor and appreciate those moments. You will always have those warm and fond memories to fall back on. You also learn from experience and will be in a better position to help others who are going through similar, if not worse, hardships and difficulties. When you learn through adversity or from suffering, then you become wiser and have a greater capacity to adapt and cope. You are able to apply practical wisdom into your life. You are stronger as you have persevered, thus transforming yourself into a more compassionate and empathetic person. This enables you to become someone who can have a positive impact in the world, performing thoughtful acts for others, while also recognizing your limitations. While no one can truly anticipate the outcome of any given situation, you are more prepared in how to react, as you have learned to adjust your expectations, behavior, and attitude. You become more mature as a result of your life experiences.

Faith helps too. It would be prudent to realize that although we all may have theological religious differences and come from different directions, we are all in this world together and need to be tolerant and respectful of each other. When there is a loss of a loved one, Harold Kushner reminds us that:

> ... *people die, but love does not die. It is recycled from one heart, from one life, to another.* (Kushner 2001)

In other words, he is saying that you can take comfort in your belief that a good and loving person, even after they die, will still be alive through others. This is similar to what Morris Schwartz stated in that loving relationships never cease even after death. It takes love and faith to make it happen.

I want to close this chapter with a beautiful excerpt about the realities of life, good and bad, from Ken Druck as he describes himself taking a long meditative walk. He climbs up a hill, reaches the top, then walks down to the beach and the ocean, looks around, and takes it all in. He appreciates everything good in the world:

*Giving thanks for things great and small, I am sometimes brought to tears. There is such beauty and abundance, all around us . . . if we simply open ourselves up to it. As I make my way home from the beach, I'm often stuck by the reality that I can't just open myself to one side; life is a package deal. Only when I open myself to life's cruel and brutal unfairness and its miraculous fairness can I begin to make peace with life as it really is.* (Druck 2013)

# Fleeting Comments

*I like living. I have sometimes been wildly, despairingly, acutely miserable, racked with sorrow, but through it all I still know quite certainly that just to be alive is a good thing.* (Agatha Christie)

*Life can be unfair at times, but that's no reason to give up on it.* (Author Unknown)

*What's done is done. What's gone is gone. One of life's lessons is always moving on. It's okay to look back and see how far you've come but keep moving forward.* (Roy T. Bennett)

*There are no guarantees. There are no promises, but there is you, and strength inside to fight for recovery. And always there is hope.* (Gilda Radner)

*My mama always said, "Life is like a box of chocolates. You never know what you're gonna get."* (Forrest Gump)

*You cannot control everything that happens to you; you can only control the way you respond to what happens. In your response is your power.* (Author Unknown)

*Nothing lasts forever, not even your troubles.* (Arnold H. Glasow)

*I believe that if life gives you lemons, you should make lemonade ... And try to find somebody whose life has given them vodka and have a party.* (Ron White)

*Life is unfair but remember, sometimes it is unfair in your favor.*
(Peter Ustinov)

# CHAPTER 32

# Being Human

*The greatness of humanity is not in being human;*
*but in being humane.* (Mahatma Gandhi)

Let's face it. Human beings have good and bad tendencies. We can be charitable and giving at times and self-centered on other occasions. We can be truthful or deceitful. We can lead a life of integrity or corruption. The main point is that good people will perform good deeds and think of others because they are good people. Likewise, people behave badly because they are human, which is not an excuse, rather an explanation.

So be careful what you wish for, particularly when you are competing in the rat race of work, wealth, and success. There is a risk that when you are totally consumed by success, you take your eye off of things that really matter. Serial entrepreneur Jeff Sandefer and Reverend Robert Sirico authored a book together where they elaborated on the dangers of being too preoccupied with such pursuits as wealth, status, and success:

*They can keep us from loving our family as we ought; can tempt us to violate our ethics and damage our integrity; can hinder us from living a full spiritual life. If we come to love success and natural wealth more than we love any-thing else—family, God, integrity—then wealth has become our master rather than our servant, an idol that we bow down to. It has conquered us.* (Sandefer and Sirico 2012)

Take advantage of the many opportunities that being human affords you. Be aware of all the beauty life has to offer. Grow into the person you desire to be. Experience life, good and bad. The highs and the lows. The bliss and the sorrow. The blessings and the pain. Through it all, commit to living a life that matters in this world so that you have not lived your life in vain. Live a life of kindness, love, integrity, and being a role model that others look up to.

Being human can sometimes be about giving away integrity, such as by cheating or stealing to get ahead. When that happens, there is a tradeoff of short-term gain or pleasure versus the knowledge that you have to live forever with the stigma that you are funda-mentally dishonest, whether you get caught or not. You will have to look at yourself in the mirror with that on your conscience. You will ultimately lose more than you gain, as there will most likely be a reckoning in this life or the next. It is not worth it and never will be. Always do what is morally right so that you never have to apologize to anyone.

All of us have a dark side and we struggle with ourselves. As humans, we are conflicted at times; but it is in our best interest to learn to work through it until we find our true values and moral compass. By doing so, it will keep us on the right path forward.

There is a biblical story about Jacob that serves to highlight the theme of being human and provides some teachable moments in today's world. Here is a very condensed synopsis.

In his younger days Jacob was known to be a trickster, deceitful, and a conniver, especially toward his twin brother Esau. After being discovered and threats were made, Jacob fled his country to live and work with his uncle. Jacob had two wives, Rachel and Leah. He eventually wanted to make amends with his brother, so he decided to return home. When he reached the border of Canaan and Aram, he sent the women, children, and animals ahead and was left alone. That night a mysterious figure attacked him, and the fight continued all night long. The attacker was as strong as Jacob, and although Jacob was bruised, he ended up being unharmed.

According to Harold Kushner, his interpretation is that the attacker is Jacob's conscience. He was at war with himself, attempting to fight off the bad impulses he had. That is the part of him that was fighting with the person he wanted to become. This experience changed his outlook and improved his attitude and life. Here is Harold Kushner analyzing this more deeply and bringing it back to everyday life:

> *I think many of us can identify with Jacob's struggle, symbolized in the biblical narrative as wrestling with an angel. There are times when we feel the split inside us, part of us wanting to take the easy way out even as another part of us insists on taking the more demanding route, part of us wanting to give money to the beggar or write a check to charity while another part of us gives us reasons to keep the money for ourselves, part of us wanting to play*

*the Good Samaritan and stop to help someone in need while a voice inside our head urges us not to get involved. There are times when we scold ourselves, How could you do that? Didn't you know it was wrong? Or warn ourselves, Stop right now and don't go any further before you get in trouble. We know how easy it is, with practice, to ignore the voice of conscience.* (Kushner 2001)

Being human means having to go through these internal conflicts within yourself at some point in your life. This is normal. Remind yourself of your core values and live your life by them. Keep your internal conflicts in check, along with your ego. You won't be held accountable for any dark inner thoughts, ideas, or feelings, but rather for how you act and what you do. Bad choices can be innocent or deliberate, but either way they can have unintended consequences that hurt others. Individuals go through different phases with different interests as they grow up and mature. Be aware of what kind of person you are. Be honest with yourself. Humans can and do evolve and change if there is enough desire to do so.

Here is another example or analogy to drive home the same point of having a dark side. You probably remember Robert Louis Stevenson's famous book *The Strange Case of Dr. Jekyll and Mr. Hyde.* In the fictitious story, Dr. Jekyll is a respected and kind doctor who has repressed evil thoughts inside of him. In an attempt to control his dark side, he develops a serum, but instead it transforms him into the evil persona of himself, Mr. Hyde. At the beginning, he transforms back and forth until eventually Mr. Hyde becomes too dominant, and he is transformed permanently into his hideous alter ego. In my opinion, the moral of the story is that if you have a looming Mr. Hyde within you, control it naturally (i.e., without drugs or alcohol) and keep it permanently bottled up. There are ways to manage stress, urges, and temptations. Try to use logic, knowledge, and practical wisdom rather than your emotions. If you are successful, your life will have more stability.

Being human can include growing out of or atoning for immature, illegal, mischievous, or poor conduct. It can also be about personal growth, freedom, love, and being a good person with good intentions. Everyone has choices to make as to what kind of life they end up living and what kind of ethics they will follow.

- Choose to take the noble high ground and resist the temptations of the morally challenged route.
- Be aware of your internal conflicts. Pause, reflect, and make life choices that align with your core values.
- Focus on being a good human and making a positive difference.
- Live your best life in the time you are alive.
- Be the kind of person others emulate.

In the long run, affirmative behavior is more constructive. You won't have to struggle with yourself or battle the angel inside your conscience. The reward is that you can look at yourself in the mirror, smile, and hold your head up. You will sleep better and maybe, and perhaps most importantly, you will be at peace with yourself.

# Mortal Messages

*As human beings, our job in life is to help people realize how rare and valuable each one of us really is, that each of us has something that no one else has—or ever will have—something inside us that is unique to all time.* (Fred Rogers)

*Live life fully while you're here. Experience everything. Take care of yourself and your friends. Have fun, be crazy, be weird. Go out and screw up! You're going to anyway, so you might as well enjoy the process. Take the opportunity to learn from your mistakes; find the cause of your problem and eliminate it. Don't try to be perfect; just be an excellent example of being human.* (Tony Robbins)

*The passion to explore is at the heart of being human.* (Carl Sagan)

*Storytelling has always been at the heart of being human because it serves some of our most basic needs; passing along our traditions, confessing failings. Healing wounds, engendering hope, strengthening our sense of community.* (Parker Palmer)

*Challenging the meaning of life is the truest expression of being human.* (Viktor Frankl)

*My therapist told me the way to achieve true inner peace is to finish what I start. So far, I've finished two bags of M&M's and a chocolate cake. I feel better already.* (Dave Barry)

## CHAPTER 33

# Gratitude and Appreciation

*Nothing else can quite substitute for a few well-chosen, well-timed, sincere words of praise. They're absolutely free and worth a fortune.* (Sam Walton)

Embrace gratitude! Be thankful for who you are and grateful for what you've got. Appreciate the righteousness in the world and block out the adversity. I know that's easier said than done since there is plenty of news going on in the world and not all of it is pretty. However, if you are able to block out and compartmentalize the noise from the news and from inside your mind, at least some of the time, things do look rosier and more promising, and your stress levels diminish.

Gratitude and appreciation matter. When you are able to appreciate your best parts of your existence and express gratitude, it conveys positive karma and energizes you and everyone around you. It is a healthy approach to life and sends a message of goodwill and enthusiasm to those you are grateful for. It sparks excitement and brings out a revised demeanor in you.

When you demonstrate your direct gratitude or appreciation to someone, it is a form of flattery, and is a compliment to the person you appreciate. Telling someone that you are grateful for who they are or what they do provides immense benefits. It makes others feel good, puts a smile on their face, and elicits a good sentiment and feeling. It makes the recipient happy. While there are different methods of communicating your gratitude and appreciation, such as giving a real or token gift, it does not cost anything to tell someone that you appreciate them or to send them a quick note or email. Age does not matter because you can appreciate someone at any age or at any time. It can be for a job well done, for a favor performed on your behalf, for anything of even minor significance, or for no reason at all.

When you compliment, thank, or express gratitude to a friend, an acquaintance, a family member, your spouse, someone you work with, or even a stranger, it is an act of kindness. It evokes a moment of joy to both the giver and the receiver of the kindness. It feels good to display genuine gratitude and appreciation.

Gratitude and appreciation are also a state of mind. It is recognition that life, with all of its shortcomings, is extraordinary. Close relationships that you forge are special and should not be diminished or taken for granted. Having the right frame of mind influences how you perceive the world around you and modifies your behavior. This mindset reshapes your attitude and reinforces your faith in humanity. This could last just in the moment, or you can work to make it more sustainable, if you immerse yourself in that mentality and make it part of your daily routine. Living a life of gratitude and appreciation is contagious and ripples into other aspects of your life. It helps with enhancing relationships, intimacy, and personal contentment, and is an affirmation of recognition and thankfulness. It can change your outlook, boost your confidence, and help to promote change and purpose.

When you are thankful, it is difficult to be hateful. Once you conclude that so much of your life has been blessed, that you are indeed fortunate and not cursed, more blessings will come your way. Those around you take notice and reciprocate by showing how grateful and appreciative they are of you.

# Truisms

*Gratitude is not only the greatest of virtues, but the parent of all others.* (Cicero)

*By taking the time to stop and appreciate who you are and what you've achieved—and perhaps learned through a few mistakes, stumbles, and losses—you actually can enhance everything about you. Self-acknowledgement and appreciation are what give you the insights and awareness to move forward toward higher goals and accomplishments.* (Jack Canfield)

*You have it easily in your power to increase the sum total of this world's happiness now. How? By giving a few words of sincere appreciation to someone who is lonely or discouraged. Perhaps you will forget tomorrow the kind words you say today, but the recipient may cherish them over a lifetime.* (Dale Carnegie)

*Think with deep gratitude of those who have lighted the flames within us.* (Albert Schweitzer)

*Develop an attitude of gratitude and give thanks for everything that happens to you, knowing that every step forward is a step toward achieving something bigger and better than your current situation.* (Brian Tracy)

*If you concentrate on finding whatever is good in every situation, you will discover that your life will suddenly be filled with gratitude, a feeling that nurtures the soul.* (Harold Kushner)

*Appreciation is a wonderful thing. It makes what is excellent in others belong to us as well.* (Voltaire)

*For me, every hour is grace. And I feel gratitude in my heart each time I can meet someone and look at his or her smile.* (Elie Wiesel)

*(Presumably while giving a thank you speech) I don't deserve this award, but I have arthritis and I don't deserve that either.* (Jack Benny)

# CHAPTER 34

# Forgiveness

*When you forgive, you heal. When you let go, you grow.*
(Author Unknown)

On May 13, 1981, Pope John Paul II was shot and seriously wounded by a Turkish militant fascist as he entered St. Peter's Square. The assailant, Mehmet Ali Ağra, was caught, arrested, and sentenced to life imprisonment. A few years later Pope John Paul II visited Ağra in jail and forgave him for his actions. At the pope's request, Ağra was later pardoned by the Italian president and extradited back to Turkey. He eventually converted to Christianity and visited the tomb of John Paul II in 2014, nine years after the Pope passed away, even putting flowers on it.

Forgiveness is about letting someone off the hook for something they have done to you. It is letting go of the judgments you made and moving on. When you continue to blame someone or something else, it is difficult to forgive and move on. Forgiving enables you to release your negative emotions and start over again. Someone like Nelson Mandela was able to forgive his oppressors in spite of all the incredible hardship he had to endure for so many years. The same for Viktor Frankl. There are countless other stories of victims or the families of victims forgiving a criminal for committing sometimes heinous crimes against them or someone close to them. In some situations, it is the victim's religious faith that provides the impetus to forgive and not to hate. It takes courage to move on. Forgiving is about demeanor and mindset. You will need to decide for yourself whether an individual, organization, or entity should or can be forgiven.

Revenge is the opposite of forgiveness, as it crowds out all the healthier and positive emotions. It might feel good, and it can make a good story or movie (examples might include *The Shawshank Redemption* or *The Count of Monte Cristo*), but it is not always virtuous. When you are obsessed with revenge or wish ill will to someone else just for the sake of it, without a legal or specific remedy, you are allowing that person or group to dominate and redirect you. They are living in your head and nothing good will happen.

When you forgive someone who did something wrong, you do it for your sake, not theirs. While you should not accept, forget, or condone the behavior or act that caused the conflict, being able to move forward is a demonstration of personal growth and maturity. The act of forgiving takes away anyone's ability to maintain control or power over you. It frees you up to persevere, press the reset button, and go on with living your life.

There are different ways to forgive. It can be done by talking, by correspondence, or in person. Sometimes it works and sometimes the conflict is irreconcilable. Everyone is human and emotions and feelings do come out. Some of you can forgive by letting go in your mind. Wipe your hands of the matter emotionally and move on. Some of you can do this while others will have a disconnect between the heart and the mind. For some of you, prayer seems to work as a spiritual way of letting go. There are times when conflicts can be resolved, especially when both sides work it out together. Compromise may need to happen, and you may have to swallow more pride than you want. Think of the end result that you desire. Sometimes the ends do justify the means.

There are times when you need to forgive yourself. Everyone makes mistakes and we can be our own harshest critics. You should acknowledge, apologize, make amends, and lose the guilt. Learn from the past and do better in the future.

It can feel good to rid yourself of bitterness and anger. Learn to detach your emotions from the situation. It is cleansing to be able to forgive. It is toxic when you want revenge and revenge is not good for your health.

Everyone has a choice in how to deal with conflict, especially those who have been pent up for a long time. Some of you may have unfavorable repressed memories or those that are too embarrassing for you to think about. The goal of this book is to make the case for you to lead a healthy and meaningful life with as much joy, laughter, and happiness as possible. Forgiveness can be part of that healing process.

Let's end this chapter with a marvelous excerpt from Jeff Sandefer and Robert Sirico about choices, forgiveness, and living a life without regrets:

> ... *making small choices that add up to a big life. A life in which you make a difference—in yourself, in others, in the world. A life in which you forgive yourself for your trespasses, knowing that you've learned from them, and*

*in which you forgive the trespasses of others. A life in which you close your eyes for the last time without regret, confident that you took the hours and days and years you were given and made something spectacular out of them.* (Sandefer and Sirico 2012)

# Forgiving Fables

*When you choose to forgive those who have hurt you, you take away their power.* (Author Unknown)

*Darkness cannot drive out darkness; only light can do that. Hate cannot drive out hate; only love can do that.* (Martin Luther King Jr)

*It's one of the greatest gifts you can give yourself, to forgive. Forgive everybody.* (Maya Angelou)

*Without forgiveness life is governed by an endless cycle of resentment and retaliation.* (Roberto Assagioli)

*Forgive your enemies, but never forget their names.* (John F. Kennedy)

*It's not just other people we need to forgive. We also need to forgive ourselves. For all the things we didn't do. All the things we should have done.* (Mitch Albom)

*Forgiveness is a funny thing. It warms the heart and cools the sting.* (Peter Allen)

*My idea of forgiveness is letting go of resentment that does not serve your better interest, ridding yourself of negative thoughts. All they do is make you miserable. Believe me, you can fret and fume all you want, but whoever it was that wronged you is not suffering from your anguish whatsoever.* (Della Reese)

*And when you stand praying, if you hold anything against anyone, forgive them, so that your Father in heaven may forgive your sins.* (Jesus Christ)

# CHAPTER 35

# Kindness

*Nothing can make our lives, or the lives of other people, more beautiful than perpetual kindness.* (Leo Tolstoy)

Kindness is a mindset. It should be the natural way in which you live your life. After all, it's following the golden rule. Treat others as you would like to be treated yourself. Give more of yourself to others; ask nothing in return. Volunteer your time or money to something or someone to cheer them up or for any reason at any time. These can be random acts of kindness, which may appear to others as being random but in fact are quite deliberate. It's just the essence of who you are. Always be nice to others and pleasant to be around. You will find that it isn't that hard to be nice.

Random acts of kindness can be small token expressions to anyone, including strangers, including saying hello, smiling, opening a door, sending a note, offering up your seat, lending a helping hand, handing out a sincere compliment, being there for a friend, or giving someone a ride. Acts of kindness could include just listening to someone during times of distress, sorrow, or despair while perhaps offering words of encouragement, strength, support, or hope.

Of course, there are monetary gestures. You can pay for a coffee, a meal, flowers, chocolate, and so on.

When you are able to give or share more of yourself to others, even in small but noble ways, people notice. What may seem inconsequential to you may be consequential to them. It can lift them up when they need lifting. Small tokens of random, unexpected kindness leave an impression on the recipients. When it makes the other party feel good, it makes you feel good. When they smile, you smile. If they laugh, you laugh. When they are happy, you are happy. The pure energy of giving doubles the amount of joy you send and receive.

When you help someone else feel better, it has a boomerang effect. It helps you feel better about yourself. It becomes contagious when others pass the random act of kindness forward. Helping someone is a great cure for when you are feeling down about your own life. Never underestimate the ability you have to make someone's day whether or not you realize it at the time. Sometimes words of encouragement or a piece of advice have a great impact on changing someone's attitude or perspective on their day. While the act may only be a moment in time, the memory and the shelf life of your act will linger longer.

It is important to recognize that while you cannot change the world on a macro scale, you can make an impact on the people around you. You have the ability to shine and make others smile and laugh. When you bring that heightened awareness into your daily routine, it becomes part of your DNA. It sparks excitement. When you have the ability to touch another person in even a subtle way, it is empowering. It is not that difficult if you repeat this simple mantra, just three words, and always live your life this way: "Just be kind!"

Kindness promotes foundational core values. These core values transform into meaning. The meaning promotes a sense of purpose. As you live a life of peace, kindness, and integrity, this adds to your life story as to who you are and the kind of person you have become. These qualities and life stories become a part of your moral autobiography and ultimate legacy. A legacy of pure kindness, giving, and sharing. How wonderful a legacy that is!

## Cordial Considerations

*Kind words can be short and easy to speak, but their echoes are truly endless.* (Mother Teresa)

*Kindness is invincible.* (Marcus Aurelius)

*Kindness in words creates confidence. Kindness in thinking creates profoundness. Kindness in giving creates love.* (Lao Tzu)

*You cannot do kindness too soon, for you will never know how soon it will be too late.* (Ralph Waldo Emerson)

*Too often we underestimate the power of a touch, a smile, a kind word, a listening ear, an honest compliment, or the smallest act of caring, all of which have the potential to turn a life around.* (Leo Buscaglia)

*I expect to pass through life but once. If therefore, there be any kindness I can show, or any good thing I can do to any fellow being, let me do it now, and not defer or neglect it, as I shall not pass this way again.* (William Penn)

*In all your life, you will never find a method more effective in getting through to another person than to make that person feel important.* (Will Rogers)

*Obey the voice within—it commands us to give of ourselves and help others. As long as we have the capacity to give, we are alive.* (Kirk Douglas)

*Carry out a random act of kindness, with no expectation of reward, safe in the knowledge that one day someone might do the same for you.* (Princess Diana)

# CHAPTER 36

# Happiness

*Those who are not looking for happiness are the most likely to find it, because those who are searching forget that the surest way to be happy is to seek happiness for others.* (Martin Luther King, Jr.)

Happiness is the holy grail of life. Everyone strives for it. Some achieve happiness in moments of time while others lead lives of extended happiness and fulfillment. By definition, happiness is the state of being happy, content, or joyful.

In Dan Buettner's book *The Blue Zones of Happiness*, Professor Edward Diener writes in the foreword as he astutely addresses the importance of happiness:

> *... happiness is an essential part of functioning well, and that it gives a boost in well-being not only to individuals, but also to those around them, their communities, and their societies. Rather than being a luxury to be pursued only after we take care of the more important things in life, happiness is beneficial to everything else we desire: It aids our health and helps us live longer; it aids our functioning*

*and makes us better citizens; it helps us perform better at work; it builds up our resilience, which enables us to bounce back after setbacks and or when bad events occur in our lives. The happier we are, the better we are for our friends and family, our workplaces, our communities, and our society as a whole.* (Buettner 2017)

He continues about the added value of happy workers in the workforce:

*The happiest people are superstars of giving support to others, which make everyone perform better. It is important for business leaders to understand that employees who enjoy their work are likely to outperform others, and that companies with many such employees are more likely to thrive.* (Buettner 2017)

So what are some of the predictors of long-term happiness? Arthur Brooks answers this question on happiness from the results of various research studies. Here is a brief synopsis:

*The researchers found that some predictors are controllable, while others aren't. Among the uncontrollable factors—uncontrollable by us, at least—are the social class of parents, having a happy childhood, having long-lived ancestors, and avoiding clinical depression ... There are seven big predictors of being happy—well that we can control directly:*

1. *Smoking. Simple: don't smoke—or at least, quit early.*
2. *Drinking. . . If there is* any *indication of problem drinking in your life, or if you have drinking problems in your family, do not wonder about it or take your chances. Quit drinking right now.*
3. *Healthy body weight. Avoid obesity. Without being fanatical, maintain a body weight in the normal range, eating in a moderate, healthy way without yo-yo diets or crazy restrictions you can't maintain over the long run.*
4. *Exercise. Stay physically active, even with a sedentary job . . .*
5. *Adaptive coping style. This means confronting problems directly, appraising them honestly, and dealing with them directly without excessive rumination, unhealthy emotional reactions, or avoidance behavior.*
6. *Education. More education leads to a more active mind later on, and that means a longer, happier life . . . it simply means lifelong, purposive learning, and lots of reading.*
7. *Stable, long-term relationships. For most, this is a steady marriage, but there are other relationships that can fit here. The point is having people with whom you grow together, whom you can count on, no matter what comes your way.* (Brooks 2012)

According to researchers, Arthur Brooks points out that the most important trait for happiness is healthy relationships. Happiness is love, and good relationships keep us happier and healthier.

In his book *Solving for Why*, Dr. Mark Shrime describes that happiness is a moving sidewalk. You need more happiness to stay happy:

*The pursuit of happiness isn't unlike addiction. They both work through analogous bio-chemical pathways. Dopamine, a reward neurotransmitter, hits our brains with a short-term boost of happiness when good things happen. Seeing the finish line at the end of a race and getting your second wind? That's dopamine. Your first kiss? Dopamine. Finding that lost sock, eating that spectacular meal, or taking the perfect picture? Also dopamine.* (Shrime 2022)

Aligning your life with your values is a hopeful path to follow. It can bring you purpose and meaning. This type of lifestyle often leads to sustainable happiness, which is analogous to a natural and healthy positive dopamine level.

Viktor Frankl points out that happiness is never a goal but an outcome. It cannot be pursued; it must ensue. Once you have meaning in your life, it not only brings happiness and joy, it also gives you the capability of coping with pain and suffering.

Matthew Kelly shares his views on sustainable happiness:

*... happiness is intimately linked to our essential purpose. In each of the four areas—physical, emotional, intellectual, and spiritual... Why do we get a deep sense of fulfillment and happiness from those activities? Because they help us fulfill our essential purpose. The activities that help us become the-best-version-of-ourselves also fill our lives with sustainable happiness.* (Kelly 1999)

Some of you find happiness and pleasure in your work. That works when you feel that you are using your abilities and not wasting your talent or abilities. Your happiness is enhanced when your abilities are appreciated, and you know that you are exerting maximum effort, are proud of the work that you do, and are satisfied with the end results of that work.

At the end of the day, short-term happiness can be achieved through temporary dopamine rushes. Sustainable happiness takes more effort and requires good habits and great relationships. I believe attitude and perspective count. Happiness is like a muscle. So is joy.

- Periodically remind yourself what a privilege it is to be alive.
- Take time to reflect, rejoice, celebrate, and savor all the goodness and blessings that exist in your life.
- Find happiness in the little moments in your life and seek to make it as everlasting as you possibly can. Every moment can be memorable and eternal.
- Appreciate the gift of life and every breath that comes with it.
- Unlock your potential, find meaning and purpose, love and be loved, and be true to yourself, and happiness will follow.

# Happy Thoughts

*The happiness of your life depends upon the quality of your thoughts.* (Marcus Aurelius)

*The healthiest response to life is joy.* (Deepak Chopra)

*Happiness is when what you think, what you say, and what you do are in harmony.* (Mahatma Gandhi)

*Even a happy life cannot be without a measure of darkness, and the word happy would lose its meaning if it were not balanced by sadness. It is far better to take things as they come along with patience and equanimity.* (Carl Jung)

*Happiness is a gift, and the trick is not to expect it, but to delight in it when it comes.* (Charles Dickens)

*True happiness is to enjoy the present, without anxious dependence upon the future, not to amuse ourselves with either hope or fears but to rest satisfied with what we have. The great blessings of mankind are within us and within our reach. A wise man is content with his lot, whatever it may be, without wishing for what he has not.* (Seneca)

*One must believe in the possibility of happiness in order to be happy.* (Leo Tolstoy)

*Happiness is like a butterfly; the more you chase it, the more it will evade you, but if you notice the other things around you, it will gently come and sit on your shoulder.* (Henry David Thoreau)

*Happiness comes from spiritual wealth, not material wealth... Happiness comes from giving, not getting. If we try hard to bring happiness to others, we cannot stop it from coming to us also. To get joy, we must give it, and to keep joy, we must scatter it.* (John Templeton)

*Happiness is not a goal...it's a by-product of a life well lived.* (Eleanor Roosevelt)

*What's the use of happiness? It can't buy you money.* (Henny Youngman)

# CHAPTER 37

# Celebrate Life

*The whole world is full of miracles, but we're so used to them we call them ordinary things.* (Hans Christian Andersen)

Life is precious. Life is a gift and so never take life for granted. Celebrate the here and now. Count your many blessings. Be thankful for all the blessings you have received and be grateful for all the pleasures bestowed onto you. Be kind to others and you may find that others will be kind to you. Have sympathy, compassion, and empathy for those who are suffering through hardships. Give when you can and serve to help others in need.

Live an inspired life. When you do, you are able to accomplish more and are able to live in the moment. Harness your energy and live up to your potential. Understand that although life is challenging and sometimes aggravating, you have no control over the world surrounding you. However, you can control your reaction to it and your attitude.

When you celebrate life, you never lose hope, and you never give up. The glass is always half full, not half empty. You are able to savor the beauty in life and capture the remarkable moments in time. So stay strong and positive. Look for opportunities to succeed and do not be afraid to fail. If you do fail, don't despair; rather, learn from it. Experience different facets that interest you. Life is about making wonderful memories, some of which are captured by pictures or videos. Remind yourself how fortunate you are to be alive.

Here is Harold Kushner about embracing simple moments in time:

> *Instead of brooding over the fact that nothing lasts, accept that as one of the truths of life, and learn to find meaning and purpose in the transitory, in the joys that fade. Learn to savor the moment, even if it does not last forever. In fact, learn to savor it because it is only a moment and will not last. Moments of our lives can be eternal without being everlasting . . . What is life about? It is not about writing great books, amassing great wealth, achieving great power. It is about loving and being loved. It is about enjoying your food and sitting in the sun rather than rushing through lunch and hurrying back to the office. It is about savoring the beauty of moments that don't last, the sunsets, the leaves turning color, the rare moments of true human communication. It is about savoring them rather than missing out on them because we are so busy and they will not hold still until we get around to them.* (Kushner 1986)

Celebrating life is a recognition that your life is a series of moments. Some will stay in your mind indefinitely. Embracing that perspective will elevate the joy and pleasures in your life. When you have the right attitude and appreciation of life, then life itself becomes your reward.

Daniel Cohen expresses his thoughts about life:

*We all have struggles. I know I do. But life is all about having a positive attitude and living each day to the fullest, so that when it is our last, we can look back with no regrets.* (Cohen 2017)

Here is a feel-good daily ritual you can do to celebrate life when you are in the company of others. You are probably doing it already over cocktails or at dinner. Pour a glass of your favorite wine (of course it can be beer, water, or beverage of choice), raise your glasses, and do a quick toast. Touch your glasses together and say something positive and upbeat. It can be meaningful, congratulatory, to honor someone or something, or just to say cheers and good wishes. It can be about gratitude and appreciation. While this only takes a few moments, it is an expression of goodwill and friendship. This simple act connects and bonds people together. It sets the right tone, makes everyone at ease in a nice frame of mind, and puts a smile on everyone's faces.

- You only live once, for tomorrow is never promised.
- Focus on what really matters and make the most of today.
- Tune out any toxicity that invades your space.
- Life is beautiful and there is so much to be grateful for. Open your eyes and take it all in.
- Spend time outdoors and breathe in the sweet aromas that the seasons provide.

- Be a positive role model and live a life of integrity.
- Stay true to your faith and core values.
- Have fun and laugh a lot.
- Lead a healthy life.
- Spend quality time with people you care about and love.
- Be sure to toast life in all its glory and all of its splendor. Never stop celebrating life!

# Euphoric References

*Be glad of life because it gives you the chance to love, to work, to play, and to look up at the stars.* (Henry Van Dyke, Jr.)

*This world, after all our science and sciences, is still a miracle: wonderful, magical, and more, to whoever will think of it.* (Thomas Carlyle)

*While we have the gift of life, it seems to me that the only tragedy is to allow part of us to die—whether it is our spirit, our creativity, or our glorious uniqueness.* (Gilda Radner)

*Live in the present and make it so beautiful that it's worth remembering.* (Arnold H Glasgow)

*Remembering that life won't last forever makes us enjoy it all the more today.* (Arthur C. Brooks)

*When I started counting my blessings, my whole life turned around.* (Willie Nelson)

*Cherish each hour of this day for it can never return.*
(Og Mandino)

*When you arise in the morning, think of what a precious privilege it is to be alive—to breathe, to think, to enjoy, and to live.*
(Marcus Aurelius)

*Learn to enjoy every minute of your life. Be happy now. Don't wait for something outside of yourself to make you happy in the future. Think how really precious is the time you have to spend, whether it's at work or with your family. Every minute should be enjoyed and savored.* (Earl Nightingale)

*There are only two ways to live your life. One is though nothing is a miracle. The other is as if everything is.* (Albert Einstein)

*What a wonderful thought it is that some of the best days of our lives haven't even happened yet.* (Anne Frank)

# CHAPTER 38

# Being Authentic

*Honesty and transparency make you vulnerable. Be honest and transparent anyway.* (Mother Teresa)

Being authentic is always being true to your core identity and convictions, no matter the case. You say what you mean, and you mean what you say. Others know that they can rely on you and that your word is your bond. With authenticity comes integrity, reliability, and a degree of humility. When you are authentic, you are able to relax and let your guard down. You are not intimidated into having others think on your behalf. You are comfortable being in your own skin. You know who you are and yet are tolerant of other viewpoints. You do not let your ego get too big, and you are not too full of yourself.

When you are authentic, you are human. You are prepared to accept pain and loss and not hide your emotions. You are able to dream, to hope, and to love. Being authentic means that you anticipate that life will throw you curveballs. Therefore, you must be mentally strong and prepared to adapt to whatever comes your way. This means being flexible and realistic.

When you are authentic, you don't lose sight of what you stand for. While you strive for financial independence, you don't get lost in the euphoria of acquiring material wealth. You focus on what's really important, knowing that fame and fortune are not really what they are made out to be. Being authentic is a top priority.

Living with authenticity means knowing who you are and being that person all the time. You don't have to pretend to be someone else or fabricate stories to make yourself sound bigger or more important than everyone else. It means being whole or undivided. It is living a life of faith, whether it is in a religious sense, having confidence in yourself, or both.

Being authentic is understanding compassion and empathy. It is putting yourself in someone else's shoes and seeing the world through their eyes. When you are more empathetic, you are sensitive to other people's fears, anguish, hopelessness, and problems. Your ability to feel what someone is feeling, to have genuine sympathy and compassion, is a signal of emotional connection to others. It is an intimate and sincere connection.

Henry Emmons and David Alter address the case for authenticity:

> *It is deeply gratifying (blissful) when you feel that being yourself is enough, and when you know that offering that to the world makes it somehow a better place. Indeed, giving back seems to be a central ingredient for joy—offering yourself to the world freely, without reserve. You may or may not be compensated for it (financially, at least), but it needs to be done nonetheless, and what comes back to you is more joy. It is not something to keep to yourself.*

*It is something to be shared with the world . . .* (Emmons and Alter 2016)

Authentic people reach out and help or mentor others without needing anything in return. It is a form of genuine kindness extended to others you come across. Being genuine is being able to listen, be present, and be a friend. There is never any hidden agenda or precondition. It is just who you are.

The value of being authentic is that other people recognize who you are and will reciprocate when you need them in your life. When something bad happens to you, they show up and they do not ask for anything in return. This is the reward for connectiveness, friendship, and intimacy. After all, we are social beings, and our lives are better off when we surround ourselves with people whom we want to be with.

Being authentic is a virtue since you do not have to pretend to be someone else and feel the obligation of submitting to peer pressure. It is about having knowledge and the wisdom to apply it. I believe that when you are authentic, you are able to enjoy life more, are able to laugh, do not always take life seriously, and are more at peace with yourself. I also believe that when you are authentic, it is easier to find purpose, to live a balanced life, and to focus with more clarity on your future, which in turn impacts your legacy.

When you are authentic, you are the real deal. You are genuine. You are sincere. You are trustworthy. You are honest. You are ethical and you are human, which means you are not perfect. You make mistakes like everyone does. You are consistently the same personality no matter what the occasion is. It is a wonderful trait to have, a great standard to uphold. You are the type of person others respect and want to be around. Always strive to be a genuine person, someone who is a true leader. When you do, you will be able to sleep better at night with the knowledge that you are always authentic.

# Being Real

*Be skeptical and think things through on your own. Listen with empathy and respond with grace.* (Author Unknown)

*Have a heart that never hardens, and a temper that never tires, and a touch that never hurts.* (Charles Dickens)

*Authenticity is a collection of choices that we have to make every day. It's about the choice to show up and be real. The choice to be honest. The choice to let our true selves be seen.* (Brené Brown)

*No legacy is so rich as honesty.* (William Shakespeare)

*To find yourself, think for yourself.* (Socrates)

*Be yourself, not your idea of what you think somebody else's idea of yourself should be.* (Henry David Thoreau)

*Be yourself—everyone else is taken.* (Oscar Wilde)

*Be the person your dog thinks you are.* (Ricky Gervais)

# PART 5

## Take Action
### (Plan, organize, and make it happen)

## CHAPTER 39

# Plan and Prioritize

*The key is not to prioritize what's on your schedule, but to schedule your priorities.* (Stephen Covey)

Changes do not happen in a vacuum. Change typically requires careful and deliberate planning. The first step is to recognize things you want to change about your life, such as adjusting eating habits, improving sleeping patterns, or reducing stress in your life. It could also be about moving toward a lifestyle tilted toward fulfilling greater purpose or legacy building. In any planning phase, it's best to conceptualize different ideas and then prioritize what you think you can handle and in what timeline.

If you are younger, your focus may be on having more balance in your life. If you are close to or in retirement, your motivation may be more aligned with purpose and legacy. It could be about planning to fill up your days in order to stay active, healthy, content, alive, and happy. Since many of you can be retired for twenty to thirty years or more, longevity planning needs to be factored into your planning. This needs to be considered from both a monetary and nonmonetary viewpoint.

Take an honest inventory of yourself and where you are in the current stage of your life. When you read Chapter 41 on self-reflection and Chapter 42 on a call to action, answer the questions to immediately help identify and guide your direction. Do not overlook your blind spots. Pay attention to what you would like to improve or brainstorm ideas you have for your future. Do not let your ego get in the way in self-analysis. Think big but be realistic in terms of defining what you will need in terms of support, education, experience, and training. What tools do you need? Who can you rely on to bounce ideas off of? You can probably take on more than you think you can. Tune out your fears, insecurities, and doubts. Stay positive. Take the time to get to know yourself better. Do not be afraid of taking some calculated risks. Live your life with strong convictions and seize each day for the opportunity of being able to change and improve your lifestyle or standard of living. Make sure your passions align with your goals. If you're going to commit to changing a habit or goal, then commit to it 100 percent. Do not just go through the motions and mail in your performance.

Put your goals in writing and be accountable to yourself for the results. Set reasonable timelines. Be self-motivated and make it happen. Track your progress and adjust your activity along the way. Do not be afraid to fail. These are sometimes the best learning experiences. Do not give up when progress is slower than you anticipate.

The bottom line is that you need to invest in yourself and your future. Embrace change because it makes you a better person when you do have success. Never stop assessing and reassessing. Life is always evolving and so must you. Sometimes we have to get out of our comfort zone and do something we have not done before. Be flexible in your planning and never stop learning. You might just be astounded by what you are capable of accomplishing. Always remember that time is your most precious commodity. Since we do not know when our time will run out, don't procrastinate. Use your time wisely. Get organized. Plan while you can. Do it now!

# Popular Priorities

*Life is like a coin. You can spend it any way you wish, but you may only spend it once.* (Lillian Dickson)

*If one advances confidently in the direction of his dreams and endeavors to live the life which he has imagined, he will meet with a success unexpected in common hours.* (Henry David Thoreau)

*Busy work does not mean real work. The object of all work is production or accomplishment and to either of these ends there must be forethought, system, planning, intelligence, and honest purpose, as well as perspiration. Seeming to do is not doing.* (Thomas Edison)

*By failing to prepare, you are preparing to fail.* (Benjamin Franklin)

*We require routine and tradition. That's order. Order can become excessive, and that's not good, but chaos can swamp us, so we drown—and that is also not good. You need to stay on the straight and narrow path.* (Jordan Peterson)

*I cannot make my days longer, so I strive to make them better.*
(Henry David Thoreau)

*To succeed today, you have to set priorities, decide what you stand for.* (Lee Iacocca)

*If you want to live a happy life, tie it to a goal, not to people or things.* (Albert Einstein)

*Time is really the only capital that any human being has, and the only thing he can't afford to lose.* (Thomas Edison)

*Hold fast to time! Use it! Be conscious of each day, each hour! They slip away unnoticed all too easily and swiftly.* (Thomas Mann)

*If you're bored with life—you don't get up every morning with a burning desire to do things—you don't have enough goals.*
(Lou Holtz)

# CHAPTER 40

# Good Habits

*The secret to your success is found in your daily routine.*
(John Maxwell)

When you are reading this book about finding your purpose, living a healthy lifestyle, and forming a legacy, it might sound easier than it really is. For example, how do you change your daily activities to incorporate better habits such as exercising or eating healthier? The first step is to set a goal for something you want to achieve, and then focus on setting up the proper actions that will lead you to your desired result. Plan and prioritize what is important to you or what you would like to accomplish or change. The next steps may be setting in motion behaviors or actions that you repeat enough times that it becomes a part of your normal subconscious routine. In other words, it becomes a habit.

Habits are a function of who you currently are. They are regular tendencies or automatic reactions to daily living. Habits are mental shortcuts. Changing your habits can help you become the person you want to be or the behavior you wish to identify with. For example, say you want to run a marathon; your first task might be to visualize becoming a runner. Then you need to develop an action plan by deliberately starting to jog more and more, to become that runner. As your body slowly builds endurance over time and as you learn the essentials of proper rest, hydration, stretching, and nourishment, you morph into becoming a marathon runner.

It is one thing to incorporate a new behavior into your daily routine, but the only reason you would stay with it is if it becomes a part of your character, personality, and identity. The more you repeat the behavior, the more the behavior is reinforced into your normal way of life. So be persistent. Don't stop. Stay disciplined and determined to improve yourself.

Sometimes the plan is to start good new habits and sometimes it is to eliminate bad ones (stop smoking). The idea is to start small and build from there. Let's say you want to get into better physical shape. Just make the first step by committing to going to a gym even if it's just for a few minutes at first. Improve by just an incremental amount each time and slowly grow into it so that it is not overwhelming. Small incremental changes make a big difference over time. It may even take a few months or years before you notice how your habits have shaped your behavior. The underlying concept is that actions need to persist over a long enough time to stick permanently and become a habit. Progress is not linear as the results that you are looking for are frequently delayed. The work is cumulatively stored. Eventually, it becomes automatic (as per Daniel Kahneman's System 1: thinking fast). So keep making tiny improvements.

Author James Clear wrote the impressive book *Atomic Habits*, in which he offers this valuable insight regarding choices:

*Making a choice that is 1 percent better or 1 percent worse seems insignificant in the moment, but over the span of moments that make up a lifetime these choices determine the difference between who you are and who you could be. Success is the product of daily habits—not once-in-a-lifetime transformations.*

*That said, it doesn't matter how successful or unsuccessful you are right now. What matters is whether the habits are putting you on the path toward success. You should be far more concerned with your current trajectory than with your current results... Your outcomes are a lagging measure of your habits. Your net worth is a lagging measure of your financial habits. Your weight is a lagging measure of your eating habits. Your knowledge is a lagging measure of your learning habits. Your clutter is a lagging measure of your cleaning habits. You get what you repeat.* (Clear 2018)

The impetus to creating a good habit or breaking a bad one is desire and emotion. Appealing to your emotions will be more motivating than appealing to rational thinking. Your emotions will get you to act. You generally will crave a result that will lead you to respond. Achieving and feeling successful will motivate you to repeat. One of the greatest threats to success is boredom, not failure. When it comes to outcomes, look more at the trendline than with your current results. Be patient, persistent, diligent, and disciplined.

To make small or substantial changes, you need to be motivated to achieve the desired outcome, which will have a lagging impact as a result of changing your habits. Stay focused on how you are trending when it comes to changes you are realizing.

There are many reasons and methods for changing your habits. There are also many fine resources available, such as *Atomic Habits*, to learn about developing a detailed process. In the context of this book, we are centered on how it can help drive you toward purpose, staying healthy, and remaining focused on legacy planning. If you feel there are necessary steps that you need to implement, then identifying what habits you wish to add or subtract is a place to start. Once you change your habits, you will change the direction of your life.

## Habit Hobnob

*Develop success from failures. Discouragement and failure are two of the surest stepping stones to success.* (Dale Carnegie)

*Successful people do what unsuccessful people are not willing to do. Don't wish it were easier; wish you were better.* (Jim Rohn)

*Do not wait; the time will never be "just right." Start where you stand, and work with whatever tools you may have at your command, and better tools will be found as you go along.* (Napoleon Hill)

*Depending on what they are, our habits will either make us or break us. We become what we repeatedly do.* (Sean Covey)

*Good things come to people who wait, but better things come to those who go out and get them.* (Abraham Lincoln)

*When we strive to become better than we are, everything around us becomes better too.* (Paulo Coelho)

# CHAPTER 41

# Self-Reflection

*Knowing yourself is the beginning of all wisdom. (Aristotle)*

Take a step back and reflect. It's a time for introspection. Close your eyes and look inward. Take a fresh and honest review of your life. Is there any aspect of your life that you could improve? Anything that you would like to accomplish? Or change? Do you have any regrets? If you're being honest with yourself, the answer will always be yes. You will always want to be better, healthier, kinder, more loving, and grateful. Now answer this question: Do you also think about living a life of meaning, of purpose, with an eye toward longevity or legacy planning? My guess is that many of you may not be deliberately accounting for this part of your life. My hope is that this book has nudged you into thinking more about this concept of holistic life planning. Recognition and awareness can be a good first step. When you are doing your self-reflection and looking at the past, the present, and the future, here are some intriguing questions for your consideration:

## *Your Purpose*

- What are you passionate about? What gets you the most excited when you wake up each day?
- Do you have something that gives your life meaning or purpose?
- What are your most important values? Does your lifestyle align with your values?
- Where does God, religion, spirituality, and faith fit into the hierarchy of your life? Does it? Should it?

## *Your Health*

- Are you living a healthy lifestyle?
- Do you eat healthy most of the time?
- Do you exercise regularly and, if so, do you feel the benefits?
- Do you get enough sleep with a regular schedule?
- Do you manage stress as effectively as you feel you should, most of the time?
- Do you regularly keep your brain active and are curious enough to continue to read and learn?
- Are you able to slow yourself down at times, when needed, to either meditate or breathe? Does it help you?
- Are you able to enjoy life, have fun, and laugh a lot?
- Do your emotions too often get the best of you or are you usually able to manage them?
- Are you able to live in the moment and pay attention to what is happening in the present?
- Do you feel that your life is well balanced and not skewed too much into any one area such as work? If it is, is it a temporary phenomenon? Is there anything you can do to change it?

## *Your Legacy*

- Do you feel you are generous enough with your time and money?
- Are you striving to or are you financially independent? Are your financial needs in order? Do you have a financial, retirement, or traditional estate plan in place?
- Does your charitable giving represent what is important to you or your family? What is your capacity to give? Would you like to give while you are living and/or after death for impact?
- Besides your family, is there anything else in the world to which or to whom you would like to leave a positive impact?
- What are the values, principles, and stories you would like to pass on to future generations?
- What do you want to be remembered for? Are you the hero of your own story?
- Do you feel that you are making a difference to someone or to society?
- What else do you want to accomplish going forward?
- What would your life look like if it really turned out well?
- Your last will and testament is your final teaching. What do you want it to say?

## *Further Insights for a Better Life*

- If you could change anything in your life, what would it be? What steps do you need to take to make these changes possible?
- What kind of person do you want to be? Are you living your best life possible?

- What are you most thankful for? Do you take the time to appreciate everything that has gone right in your life instead of counting your misfortunes?
- Are you a giving and forgiving person?
- Do you ever initiate and perform random acts of kindness for others without preconditions or expecting something in return?
- Do you feel that you express your love enough to those friends and family that you are close to?
- Is there more you can do to open up your heart to your community or the world around you?

### *Take Action*
- Do you take the time to identify and truly prioritize what is most important to you?
- Are there habits you wish to add or subtract from your life? If so, what are they?

Self-reflection includes revisiting your frames of reference and perceptions of everything from where your head is currently to where you want it to be. To approach this subject from a different angle, I want to share something I wrote in the summer of 2020 during the height of Covid. The publication *The Epoch Times* was about to start a new weekly series of articles entitled "Dear Next Generation," expressing the sentiment of readers. The concept was to disseminate messages or words of advice the readers would like to convey to future generations. The subject matter immediately resonated with me as it made me deliberate in a self-reflecting mode. Writing this required some introspection, but ultimately the end result felt pure and cleansing. I wrote this piece in a few hours, submitted it, and then received a response shortly after. This was the very first article published in the series. Here it is, exactly how it was written and published in 2020.

This advice is timeless and will never change from generation to generation. It is easy to say but more difficult to do and continue to do. It revolves around basic common sense, logic, and love. Here is my advice to everyone in one short sentence. *Always remember the past, live in the present, and plan for your future.* Now here are the details.

*Always remember the past.* Embrace the good and learn from the bad. Remember those who sacrificed so much and paved the way to allow you to succeed. We all make mistakes. Understand and accept them as teachable moments that have allowed you to grow as a person. Honor and celebrate your ancestors and loved ones.

*Live in the present.* Be humble, fair, and kind to others. Have compassion and empathy to those who are suffering or in pain. Be considerate and tolerant of opposing viewpoints. Be a problem solver and not a complainer. Help others whom you can help. Be a positive influence on those around you. Be in the moment when others need you and be a good listener. Commit to a lifetime of learning and being a better version of yourself. Be charitable if you are able. Lose the hate and be grateful for what is wonderful in life. Use more logic and less emotion to evaluate situations and in making decisions. Be an independent deep thinker and self-reliant. Have some balance in your life. Follow a heathy lifestyle and manage your stress properly. Keep the faith and maintain your composure. Tune out the noise and the poison all around you. Have fun and laugh!

*Plan for the future.* Use your past experiences and your present to draw upon. Dream and have a vision of your future. Be realistic and honest about it. Settle on a path forward. Do not compromise your core values to achieve your goals. Embrace education. Pay attention to the details. Budget properly and save for retirement. Seek out help when you need it. Do not be afraid to fail because it can be a valuable life lesson in the long term. If you fail, do not feel sorry for yourself. Instead, pick yourself up and start over. Never forget where you came from and continue to learn from the past. Be honest to yourself and everyone you meet. Stay positive even in darker times and keep everything in perspective. There are always others who are worse off than you. Remain hopeful and take control of whatever direction your life is headed to.

Self-reflection is a time to sit back and evaluate. Keep reassessing and reflecting on these questions periodically throughout your life. Use it as a time to reset your goals and your path forward. It is a time to plan and prioritize, to subtract habits you wish to eliminate or add habits you wish to obtain. It is about recognizing and working toward your future destiny and living your best life.

Self-reflection is soul searching and self-examination. It is when you can contemplate a grand retrospective about your life and lifestyle. In other words, are you able to extract purpose and meaning? Have you learned important lessons along the way? Have you grown as a person? Are you satisfied with the knowledge you have attained? Will you pass your hard-earned wisdom on to your loved ones or on to others?

Ultimately, what everyone wants and what matters most is that you have inner peace, comfort, and confidence that at the end of the day, *You have loved and been loved; you have lived* your *best life, a life that mattered,* and that you were able to *Make It a Life Worth Living*!

## Reflective Thinking

*Whoever doesn't know it must learn and find by experience that "a quiet conscience makes us strong."* (Anne Frank)

*I have learned over the years that when one's mind is made up, this diminishes fear. Knowing what must be done does away with fear.* (Rosa Parks)

*Within you is a stillness and a sanctuary to which you can retreat at any time and be yourself.* (Hermann Hesse)

*Self-reflection is necessary to dig beneath our own layers and visit the inner crevices of our heart and mind to develop an understanding of life.* (Author Unknown)

*Dwell not on the faults and shortcomings of others. Instead, seek clarity about your own.* (Buddha)

*When we recall the past, we usually find that it is the simplest things—not the great occasions—that in retrospect give off the greatest glory of happiness.* (Bob Hope)

*Your greatest self has been waiting your whole life; don't make it wait any longer.* (Steve Maraboli)

*If you cannot find peace within yourself, you will never find it anywhere else.* (Marvin Gaye)

*Excellence is not a destination: it is a continuous journey that never ends.* (Brian Tracy)

*It takes courage and wisdom to acknowledge there are areas you could improve. Only in identifying your limitations can you stretch yourself beyond them.* (Roy T. Bennett)

# CHAPTER 42

# A Call to Action

*How wonderful it is that nobody need to wait a single moment before starting to improve the world.* (Anne Frank)

I am extrapolating the meaning of the wonderful quote above by Anne Frank to imply that you have the power to improve yourself at any moment in time, and by doing so you are improving the world immediately surrounding you and beyond. This chapter hopes to give further guidance to identify and make those improvements because no successful self-help book would be complete without providing a methodology for actual self-improvement. The objective here is to help you gauge where you are in your life and to steer you into the direction of where you want to go. In order to generate any improvements and make your life more of a life worth living, it is imperative to first honestly assess yourself and use it as a frame of reference. The next step is to get your highest and purest convictions in writing so you have a permanent record that you can revisit in the future. Your writing becomes a journal or diary into who you are, what you value, and how you think and perceive life. The third step (although it can be done concurrently while you write) is to convert higher-priority issues into a concrete action plan.

Please keep in mind that in all of this self-analysis, there are no wrong answers and no one is going to pass judgment on you. These exercises are merely stepping stones in order to lead you down a path to your desired outcome. It is recommended that you block out the time, look in the mirror, and take a deeper dive into some important lifestyle topics that perhaps you have glossed over or even never paid attention to before.

# Rate yourself

*When love and skill work together, expect a masterpiece.*
(John Ruskin)

There have been many questions raised in the course of this book, particularly in Chapter 41 on self-reflection. Use this section as a quantitative adjunct to the qualitative questions in that and other chapters to really figure out where you stand in relation to important life, motivational, and behavioral categories. Begin by rating yourself on a scale of 1-3 using the following scoring method:

- 1 = Need to work on; you feel there is some deficiency
- 2 = Good for now; not perfect but okay enough
- 3 = Have this under control; no further action is necessary

For areas that you believe you are borderline or somewhere in between, use a rating of 1.5 or 2.5. Now let's get started with the following twenty-five statements. Be brutally honest in assessing yourself regardless of what stage in life that you are in:

1–Knowing your purpose and having passion in your life.

2–Knowing what you would like to accomplish with a clear vision going forward.

3–Being satisfied with all your accomplishments up to this point in your life.

4–Not giving up when things go wrong.

5–Knowing where and how faith and religion fit into your priorities and everyday life.

6–Having a positive attitude the vast majority of the time.

7–Having perspective at all times for what matters the most and not getting wrapped up in daily unnecessary drama. Being able to stay above the minutiae of trivial details.

8–Being there for friends and family when they need you the most.

9–Being able to bounce back quickly when life is unfair.

10–Committing to doing enough for living a healthy lifestyle.

11–Effectively managing your stress levels most of the time.

12–Being able to contain your emotions and not lose control of yourself.

13–Staying in the moment and not mentally wandering off somewhere else.

14–Having compassion and empathy for others in need and then acting on it.

15–Truly having love in your heart even when someone disappoints you.

16–Actively implementing nonmonetary legacy planning.

17–Being dedicated to always learning and honing your skills.

18–Expressing gratitude and appreciation every day and not taking life for granted.

19–Effectively forgiving those who have upset or angered you.

20–Being kind to others at all times.

21–Being humble enough to recognize your faults and sincerely apologizing when needed.

22–Being charitable enough either in terms of time, effort, or money without needing or asking for anything in return.

23–Taking time each day to celebrate something that is good about life.

24–Setting goals for yourself in any of these areas with reasonable timelines and accountability.

25–Being authentic in how you lead your life while having few regrets.

Now add up the numbers in each of these areas so you have a total score. On an overall basis, your scores will fall somewhere between 25 (1 for each topic; an unlikely score for anyone and obviously not good) to 75 (3 for each topic, which is perfect; again, unlikely if you are completely honest). The mean would be 50, which indicates that there are probably several 1 or 1.5 scores that should be addressed. If you fall above 60, you are generally in good shape in most areas. Don't be discouraged if your rating is lower than you would like in some areas. Instead, consider this as a challenge to advance and upgrade your lifestyle and standard of living. Stay upbeat and embrace any opportunity to help boost your morale, skills, and love of life.

I would recommend that you reassess yourself periodically to compare results. Since this analysis is subjective, your analysis or self-awareness may drift somewhat over time.

## Write It Out

*In order to write about life first you must live it.*
(Ernest Hemingway)

Getting your deepest and most intimate thoughts in writing provides a safe space to memorialize who you are at that specific moment in time. If taken seriously, it becomes a worthwhile exercise of meaningful self-reflection. Be sure to date your writing and your rating scores because it may be interesting for you to compare how your critical thinking evolves over time.

The following are some writing assignments for you. Before you start, here are some helpful tips. If you find that these topics are too overwhelming, try taking baby steps forward and focus on just one topic at a time so that the task at hand is small enough to comfortably assimilate. Start by gathering your sentiments and feelings and then start writing to capture your innermost thoughts while they are still fresh in your mind. Relax and let your mind go free as you continue to brainstorm. Simply let all your thoughts flow out of your head naturally and try not to embellish anything at this point. Be cognizant of any biases you have and try to minimize them, as they may take you down a different and unproductive rabbit hole. Get all your ideas out in written form no matter how absurd or random they may seem. You can refine, edit, eliminate, and proofread everything later. If writing is too difficult for you, an alternative would be to record yourself and then perhaps transcribe it later into written format.

Here are the writing topics:

* Define what your purpose is and write it out. In other words, what gets you excited when you wake up each day? What drives your inner self? If there is a gap between your dreams and reality, how can you fill that gap?
* What would you like to accomplish in the future and what new adventures would you like to experience?
* Name areas in your life that you would like to improve. Examples could be something like sleeping better or managing stress. Pick two or three of those areas at first and focus on what specific action steps you need to take to make improvements. Use the results from the first part of this chapter to help you identify them. Also reference any corresponding chapters to give you some further direction.
* Write your moral autobiography. What do you want it to say? What values, traditions, and principles are most important to you? Share all of it with your loved ones, when you are comfortable.
* Write positive affirmations about your life. If you want, you can consolidate some of these into your moral autobiography:

- What you enjoy doing the most
- What has gone right in your life
- Excellent decisions you have made that you are most proud of
- Your favorite memories either as a child or an adult
- Someone you have always looked up to as a role model and why
- Your funniest memories or stories

- The most cherished and/or toughest lessons you have experienced
- The most valuable life lessons that you learned from your parents and extended family
- The most important nonmonetary legacies you would like to leave to your children, grandchildren, or the next generation

* Take the time to seriously contemplate the questions in Chapter 41 on self-reflection. Put your answers in writing so you have a foundation or benchmark baseline of your thought process at that specific moment in time.

Another option is to write your memoirs utilizing independent companies that keep you organized and on track. One company prompts you to answer life questions over a period of time, and upon completion your writing is bound and converted into a hardcover book. It becomes your moral autobiography to share with your loved ones.

Writing can sometimes take you to unexpected yet delightful places that you could not have imagined beforehand. With the right mindset, you might find these exercises to be therapeutic. Review your writings from time to time to make sure that nothing dramatic has changed in your philosophy or analysis. Keep all your writing in an accessible, permanent file with your other important documents, perhaps in both a printed paper format and a saved online folder.

# Take Action

*Dreams don't work unless you take action. The surest way to make your dreams come true is to live them.* (Roy T. Bennett)

The next phase is planning and then acting on those plans. What areas in your life do you want to change? If there are several, what are your highest priorities? When you decide, make a list and get it down in writing.

While rating yourself and writing are forms of action, there are other tangible forms of action that vary in their degree of difficulty. Some changes, like meditating or deep breathing, can be simple to undertake. Other changes, like focusing on being in the moment, are more intangible and may be more difficult to objectively measure progress. Eating healthier and exercising consistently generally can be longer time commitments that require more intentional planning and discipline to acquire and maintain as healthy habits.

Use all the information you have acquired from this chapter and beyond to help contemplate, shape, and formalize a call to action. Decide what attributes or elements you would like to change, add, or subtract in your life. Start to organize, outline, and implement the necessary adjustments to make them happen. Keep a spreadsheet or checklist of goals, action steps taken, what you are working on, any open items, and what you have accomplished. Consider factoring in reasonable timelines, when needed, to prevent any prolonged procrastination or apathy from settling in. You may want to also reference Chapters 39 (Plan and Prioritize) and 40 (Good Habits) as a motivating resource. Use the personal note section at the back of the book (for those who have the printed book) to give yourself some additional writing space to jot down some ideas.

The financial advisor in me would like to remind you that certain goals such as extensive travel, vocational or recreational aspirations, and charitable giving will probably require some monetary planning. When they do, please budget properly for them, know your financial limitations, and spend within your means. Seek professional assistance if you need to.

You should take comfort in the fact that recognizing your deficiencies and being committed to putting in the hard work for self-improvement is an act of wisdom, maturity, and personal growth. It takes desire, fortitude, and perseverance to make real changes last. Also bear in mind that while you can share your vision and goals with a friend or loved one or have them coach or cheer you on, you are primarily accountable just to yourself. Do your best because at the end of the day, this is about your life. Make your effort a labor of love, have fun with it, and keep your eye on the endgame. Be genuine in your approach and let the real you shine through. Ultimately, the benefits you receive will greatly exceed your efforts. The eventual reward will be a renewed recognition of what is really important as well as a more fulfilling life as it pertains to purpose, health, and legacy. Success may be incremental and small at first but it will come. Please have patience and faith in the process, and never give up on yourself when there are setbacks.

Finally, thank you once again for reading my book. I truly wish you good fortune on your personal journey. May your future be bright and joyous and all of your tomorrows be filled with robust purpose, the best of health, and a legacy to be celebrated!

# Make It a Life Worth Living

A good night sleep, so underrated; it's magical,
the benefits are understated

When you wake up, seize the day; have a plan, know your way

Move your body, keep it going; rise and shine,
get the juices flowing

Activate your mind, start your brain; think independently,
it will keep you sane

Be mindful of what you eat, what you drink;
be prudent and smart, stop and think

Exercise, move around; have a routine, make it sound

Track your progress, be accountable to yourself;
stay disciplined, it won't happen by itself

Wash your body, keep it clean; brush your teeth,
maintain good hygiene

Take control of your life and watch your health;
remember it's your greatest wealth

Manage your stress, get plenty of rest; stay calm and cool,
do not get depressed

If you are stressed, or having a meltdown; meditate or
breathe slowly, to slow yourself down

Work hard, play hard, really mix it up; have some balance
in your life, really shake it up

Save some money, nice and slow; give it time, watch it grow

Invest carefully, watch your cash flow; live within your means,
seek aid for what you don't know

Have some fun, keep it light; laugh a lot, do it right

Be there for others, try to be present; live in the moment,
always be pleasant

Look at your role models, see their best traits;
gain what you can, then emulate

Find your purpose, see it through; never give up, make it come true

A positive attitude, it's yours to choose; with it so much to gain,
without it so much to lose

Keep your faith, stay true to your core; keep your head up,
your feet on the floor

Life is unpredictable, with curves and collisions;
be prepared to react, make good decisions

Be a positive role model, one with integrity;
share what you know, do it sensibly

Love and be loved, have a kind heart; help others in need,
please do your part

Learn to forgive, be humble and kind; be authentic and real,
keep your values aligned

Compassion and sympathy, like one should expect;
maintain your dignity, show some respect

Commit to lifelong learning, it is healthy and norm;
do it long enough, good habits will form

Knowledge is power, such a natural high; you also need wisdom,
to have knowledge applied

When life turns dark, becomes unfair; remember you
have loved ones, those who care

Much to appreciate, many things do go right; hang in there,
your future is bright

Forgive yourself, when you make a mistake; you are human,
give yourself a break

Contemplate your passions, and your life stories;
look back at your life, with all of its glories

Reflect on your legacy, what do you see? how will you
be remembered? what will it be?

You can reshape your destiny, change your fate;
switch direction, it's not too late

Plan your future, plot it out; be charitable when you can,
it's what life's about

Keep on dreaming, never lose hope; to lift up your spirits,
to help you cope

Embrace inner peace, you do have a choice;
you can be angry, or you can rejoice

Make marvelous memories, start now, don't wait;
seek to be happy, take time to celebrate

Because life is short, it goes by fast; in the blink of an eye,
it's all in the past

Push your boundaries, do it longer; rise to the challenge,
it makes you stronger

Be grateful with what you've got, thankful for who you are;
you are unique, you are a star

Take the time, leave enough space; live your best life,
age with grace

You only live once, don't waste it away;
cherish each moment, cherish each day

Because the evidence is clear, it is quite empirical;
that life is a gift, life is a miracle

So live your life with love, a life of giving; a wonderful life,
*Make It a Life Worth Living*!

**Barry Moschel**

# Lessons I Have Learned

*The soul that is within me no man can degrade.*
(Frederick Douglass)

In the course of researching and writing this book, I have had the opportunity to contemplate my own life story. A lot has crossed my mind as this has been a therapeutic process. I have learned a lot about myself and the world around me. While I agree with Morris Schwartz that a part of me remains at the different ages I once was, from throughout childhood, to young adult, to middle age, and to the older age I am now. I also acknowledge that there has been an evolution along the way.

Earlier in life, while I was acquiring basic and some advanced knowledge about topics such as the arts and sciences, learning how to learn, and other practical matters, I did not have the maturity and the life experience that I believe I have now. Although I would like to say that I have applied some practical wisdom along the way, I have moments when it disappears, and any wisdom regresses to a level of absolute cluelessness. I attribute my shortcomings to being human while also acknowledging my faults. During these moments,

I have strived to recognize the importance of remaining humble, learning and growing from missteps, and moving forward. I have a vision and desire to always be a better version of myself every day.

In my life, I try to practice what I preach. Here is a summary of some lessons I have learned:

As I am aging, I have realized that taking care of my mental and physical health is a part-time job. Being disciplined is a critical component of all aspects of daily living. This includes everything covered in the health section of this book. Making time to stretch and exercise is something I don't compromise on. I start my daily routines at home first thing in the morning.

I also go through some mental and breathing exercises during my exercise time. Among the hundreds of wonderful and down-to-earth quotes in the book, I repeat dozens of them to myself each day. I do it to wake up my brain, to remind myself that these are great attributes that I want to live by. I find that as I repeat these, they become my mantras. I want to incorporate these as part of my con-science. It is interesting that it is during these moments that I find my mind wandering in a creative way. I remember things I need to do, issues I need to solve, and topics, phrases, ideas, edits, or words I want to include in this book. I take notes as these topics just pop in my head. This is also my quiet, self-reflective, and spiritual time.

I have learned the importance of a good night's sleep, maintaining a regular schedule, and methods that help me fall asleep or get back to sleep. It also helps to have a really good bed.

All of us have a dark side to us that we need to control. We have all made mistakes in life along the way. I have worked hard to maintain control over any negative emotions I feel. This is an area that I feel conflicted with at times. I believe that a part of my occupation is to analyze and stay current on matters related to financial markets and economic, business, and global events so that I can answer questions and advise clients and friends. Macro decisions impact households on a micro level. In the course of evaluating trends and data, I have come to realize that these topics can sometimes make my head explode, as I question the decision-making process and judgments that are made by various political and business leaders. As more and more of this information is embedded into my mind, it can become quite distressing.

I have learned that in order to offset the negativity and darkness, I need to then shift my thoughts and remind myself of everything that is good in the world, including many wonderful friends, family, and other great people that I am fortunate to have in my life. There are also plenty of solid decision-makers, innovators, entrepreneurs, and good leaders around. When I realize this and check myself, I am able to balance my emotions, have restraint, rise above the noise, and stay rational, hopeful, realistic, and positive.

Over my lifetime, I have come to realize who I am and identify what my basic core values are. I understand that sometimes in life things are not what they appear to be. It's at those moments that I have learned to step back, gather more information, and then do some critical independent thinking. By doing so, it's not difficult to differentiate good from bad, right from wrong.

I realize the importance of respecting other people and being considerate of their feelings even if we disagree on issues. My underlying philosophy is: "You do you and I'll do me. We will then get along fine."

Aside from occasionally indulging in too much dark chocolate and gelato, I am able to resist dark or decadent temptations. I drink in moderation and stay in control of myself. In fairness, can you blame me for chocolate and gelato? With that being said, sometimes it is more than occasional. Just saying.

I totally respect the marvelous facets of faith and various religions. At its best, it brings people together as a community and provides common values to lead a life of greater morality. It showcases the importance of being a good and kind neighbor, staying grounded, and believing in something greater than yourself. In the course of researching and writing this book, I have discovered that my own spirituality and faith in God has evolved and gotten stronger.

Laughter and comedy keeps me sane. After all, life can be hilarious at times. I love to laugh and make others laugh. When we laugh, it lightens the mood, spreads joy, and makes everyone smile. It's fun, and we all need as much fun as we can in our lives. Good spirits can prevent us from sometimes taking life too seriously, when we should keep it light and easy. I also learned that not every joke works as well as I think it should. That won't stop me from trying, though.

I have learned the importance of having the right attitude. When I am too negative, I drag everything down around me. It becomes so depressing that I do not even want to be around myself. So attitude is key. I feel that when I am more positive, I am more likable and fun to be around.

Random acts of kindness can make a difference to everyone, even to strangers. You never know when someone is having a bad day and something I say or do has a positive impact. Karma matters, and what comes around goes around. As I stated earlier in the book, it does not take much of an effort to incorporate kindness into my daily life.

Being generous is something that has always been important to both my wife Ruth and me. It can be either in time, money, or just being there to listen, care, and show support.

I have learned that I love to read, write, learn, and teach. It is healthy to stay curious, flexible, and authentic. I love a good story and use storytelling as a teachable or relatable communication tool. A good story has a hero and villain, a good dramatic theme, and a moral. Old movies, television shows, or songs can be used to make a point, entertain, or just have fun with.

Here are some additional valuable lessons I have learned:

Be grateful and appreciative of every blessing I have had. Take nothing for granted as life can change abruptly. Love is one of the most important ingredients of sustained happiness. It is important to recognize when I am wrong about something and to sincerely apologize. I have improved at forgiving others when they are wrong, even when they don't admit it.

Having compassion, sympathy, and empathy for others who are going through hardships, tragedy, or loss is a trait that is ingrained in my core being. I feel that everyone should leave room in their heart for good wishes and prayer, at the very least.

As you know by now, purpose and meaning have become a higher priority for me the last few years. Life is an adventure for all of us, and we will have to continue to figure it out as we get older. Writing this book for others, charity, and my legacy has motivated and excited me. While there is a degree of altruism and paying it forward, I recognize that there is also an element of self-esteem. I attempt diligently to always keep my ego in check and not be too full of myself.

I have learned lessons from observing behaviors and actions of other people. Thus, I am better prepared to distinguish between life choices that I want to emulate and those I want to eliminate. High moral and ethical standards keep me on right track in making daily life choices. I owe much of these standards to so many people, past and present, who have taught, shaped, and helped me become who I am now. I am forever grateful to each of them. My daily overall lifestyle goal is to live a life of integrity and be a positive role model. I now take every opportunity that I can to celebrate life. With that type of outlook and clarity, life is truly wonderful!

# CHAPTER REFERENCES

**Chapter 1: Why Having Purpose Is Important**

Matthew Kelly, *The Rhythm of Life* (Beacon Publishing, 1999), 77-78.

    Ibid., 339.

Mitch Albom, *Tuesdays with Morrie* (Random House, 1997), 71.

Dan Buettner, *The Blue Zones*, Second Edition (National Geographic, 2012), 584-595.

**Chapter 2: Viktor Frankl**

Viktor Frankl, *Yes to Life* (Beacon Press, 2020), 43.

Viktor Frankl, *Man's Search for Meaning* (Beacon Press, 2006), 145-146.

    Ibid., 82-83.

**Chapter 3: Nelson Mandela**

Jeff Sandefer and Rev. Robert Sirico, *A Field Guide for the Hero's Journey* (Action Institute, 2012), 196-197.

Chris Scott, *The Simple Guide to Nelson Mandela* (TSGT Publishing, 2011).

Nelson Mandela Centre of Memory, "Biography," mandeladaypledge.org/biography/.

**Chapter 4: Charles Krauthammer**

Charles Krauthammer, *Things That Matter* (Crown Publishing Group, 2013), 22-23.

    Ibid., 435-436.

**Chapter 5: Faith and Religion**

Matthew Kelly, *The Rhythm of Life* (Beacon Publishing, 1999), 147, 150.

Rabbi Harold Kushner, *Nine Essential Things I Learned About Life* (Alfred A. Knopf, 2015), 65.

    Ibid., 89.

Rabbi Daniel Cohen, *What Will They Say About You When You Are Gone?* (Health Communications, 2017), 146.

**Chapter 7: Never Give Up**

Winston Churchill, "Never Give In" speech, www.school-for-champions. com>speeches>churchill.

**Chapter 8: Find Your Path**

Dr. Mark Shrime, *Solving for Why* (Hachette Book Group, 2022), 105.

Matthew Kelly, *The Rhythm of Life* (Beacon Publishing, 1999), 70, 71.

**Chapter 10: Eat**

David Sinclair, PhD, AO, *Lifespan: Why We Age and Why We Don't Have To* (Atria Books, 2019), 246, 261, 262, 267.

Dr. Joseph Mercola, *Fat for Fuel* (Hay House, 2017).

Jack Challem and Ron Hunninghake, MD, *Stop Prediabetes Now* (John Wiley & Sons, 2007).

Chris Johnson, *On Target Living* (John Wiley & Sons, 2013).

Max Lugavere, *Genius Foods* (HarperCollins, 2018).

**Chapter 11: Exercise**

Chris Johnson, *On Target Living* (John Wiley & Sons, 2013), 236.

Ilchi Lee, *I've Decided to Live 120 Years* (Best Life Media, 2017), 124.

David Sinclair, PhD, AO, *Lifespan: Why We Age and Why We Don't Have To*, (Atria Books, 2019), 277, 278, 282.

Henry, Emmons, MD and David Alter, PhD, *Staying Sharp* (Simon & Schuster, 2016), 132-133.

**Chapter 12: Sleep**

Chris Johnson, *On Target Living* (John Wiley & Sons, 2013), 77, 78.

Matthew Kelly, *The Rhythm of Life* (Beacon Publishing, 1999), 357, 358, 359, 360.

Max Lugavere, *Genius Foods* (HarperCollins, 2018).

**Chapter 13: Stimulate Your Brain**

Daniel Kahneman, *Thinking Fast and Slow* (Farrar, Straus, and Giroux, 2011).

Henry Emmons, MD, and David Alter, PhD, *Staying Sharp* (Simon & Schuster, 2016), 305, 317.

**Chapter 14: De-stress**

Chris Johnson, *On Target Living* (John Wiley & Sons, 2013), 64.

Skye Girard, *The Anti-Anxiety & Stress Management Handbook* (Good Vibes Publishing, 2015), 65-66.

Nick Hoff, *Stress-Free for Good* (Draft2Digital, 2019).

## Chapter 15: Breathe and Meditate
Andrew Weil, MD, *Healthy Aging* (First Anchor Books, 2005), 533.
  Ibid., 535.
Rabbi Daniel Cohen, *What Will They Say About You When You Are Gone?* (Health Communications, 2017), 80.

## Chapter 16: Laugh
Norman Cousins, *Anatomy of an Illness as Perceived by the Patient* (Open Road Integrated Media, 1979), 70, 137.
Ace McCloud, *Laughter Therapy* (Pro Master Publishing, 2017), 15.
  Ibid., 35, 38-39.

## Chapter 17: Watch Your Emotions
Jennifer Smith, *How to Control Your Emotions* (self-published, 2020), 36-37.
Andrew Weil, MD, *Healthy Aging (First Anchor Books,* 2005), 551-552.

## Chapter 18: Be Present
Henry Emmons, MD, and David Alter, *Staying Sharp* (Simon & Schuster, 2016), 107.
Ken Druck, PhD, *The Real Rules of Life* (Hay House, 2013), 71.
Rabbi Daniel Cohen, *What Will They Say About You When You Are Gone?* (Health Communications, 2017), 88-90.
  Ibid., 113.

## Chapter 20: Live Longer
Dan Buettner, *The Blue Zones*, Second Edition (National Geographic Society, 2012), 540-541.

## Chapter 21: Age Gracefully
Ilchi Lee, *I've Decided to Live 120 Years* (Best Life Media, 2017), 33.
Mitch Albom, *Tuesdays with Morrie* (Random House, 1997), 168, 169, 172.
Andrew Weil, MD, *Healthy Aging* (Random Books, 2005), 609-610.

## Chapter 22: What Everyone Wants
Ilchi Lee, *I've Decided to Live 120 Years* (Best Life Media, 2017), 52.

## Chapter 23: Traditional Estate vs. Legacy Planning
Perry Cochell and Rod Zeeb, *Beating the Midas Curse* (Allegiance Publishing, 2014), 190.
Charles Collier, *Wealth in Families* (Harvard University, 2012).
Mark Weber, *The Legacy Spectrum* (Vinton Street Press, 2017).

**Chapter 24: Your Moral Autobiography**
Scott Fithian and Todd Fithian, *The Right Side of the Table* (FPA Press, 2007), 105.
Ken Druck, PhD, *The Real Rules of Life* (Hay House, 2013), 200.

**Chapter 25: Friends and Family**
Charles Collier, *Wealth in Families* (Harvard University, 2012).
Perry Cochell and Rod Zeeb, *Beating the Midas Curse* (Allegiance Publishing, 2014), 228-230.

**Chapter 26: Tragedy and Death**
Viktor Frankl, *Yes to Life* (Beacon Press, 2020), 69-70.
Ilchi Lee, *I've Decided to Live 120 Years* (Best Life Media, 2017), 54.
Rabbi Harold Kushner, *When All You've Ever Wanted Isn't Enough* (Pocket Books, 1986), 155-156.
Ken Druck, PhD, *The Real Rules of Life* (Hay House, 2013), 69.

**Chapter 27: Knowledge and Wisdom**
Barry Schwartz and Kenneth Sharpe, *Practical Wisdom* (Penguin Group, 2011), 16.
Ibid., 403.

**Chapter 28: Love**
Arthur Brooks, *From Strength to Strength* (Penguin Random House, 2012), 343.
Mitch Albom, *Tuesdays with Morrie* (Random House, 1997), 188.
Ibid., 244.
Elisabeth Kübler-Ross and David Kessler, *On Grief and Grieving* (Scribner, 2005), 461, 463-464.

**Chapter 29: Being Charitable vs. Philanthropic**
Charles Collier, *Wealth in Families* (Harvard University, 2012).
Mark Weber, *The Legacy Spectrum* (Vinton Street Press, 2017).

**Chapter 30: What Matters Most**
Scott Fithian and Todd Fithian, *The Right Side of the Table* (FPA Press, 2007), 106-107.

**Chapter 31: Life Is Complicated, Unfair, Yet Totally Fair**
Rabbi Harold Kushner, *Living a Life That Matters* (First Anchor Books, 2001), 154.
Ken Druck, PhD, *The Real Rules for Life* (Hay House, 2013), 48.
Rabbi Harold Kushner, *When Bad Things Happen to Good People* (Schocken Books, 1981).

**Chapter 32: Being Human**
Jeff Sandefer and Rev. Robert Sirico, *A Field Guide for the Hero's Journey* (TSGT Publishing, 2012), 225.
Rabbi Harold Kushner, *Living a Life That Matters* (First Anchor Books, 2001), 27-28.

**Chapter 33: Gratitude and Appreciation**
Dr. Robert Emmons, PhD, *The Little Book of Gratitude* (Gaia Books, 2016).

**Chapter 34: Forgiveness**
Jeff Sandefer and Rev. Robert Sirico, *A Field Guide for the Hero's Journey* (TSGT Publishing, 2012), 10.
Rabbi Harold Kushner, *Living a Life That Matters* (First Anchor Books, 2001).

**Chapter 35: Kindness**
Rabbi Daniel Cohen, *What Will They Say About You When You Are Gone?* (Health Communications, 2017).

**Chapter 36: Happiness**
Dan Buettner, *The Blue Zones of Happiness* (National Geographic National Geographic Partners, 2017), 18-19.
    Ibid., 19.
Arthur Brooks, *From Strength to Strength* (Penguin Random House, 2022), 219-220.
Dr. Mark Shrime, *Solving for Why* (Hachette Brook Group, 2022), 327.
Viktor Frankl, *Man's Search for Meaning* (Beacon Press, 2006).
Matthew Kelly, *The Rhythm of Life* (Beacon Publishing, 1999), 73.

**Chapter 37: Celebrate Life**
Rabbi Harold Kushner, *When All You've Ever Wanted Isn't Enough* (Pocket Books, 1986), 141-142.
Daniel Cohen, *What Will They Say About You When You Are Gone?* (Health Communications, 2017), 164.

**Chapter 38: Being Authentic**
Henry Emmons, MD, and David Alter, PhD, *Staying Sharp* (Simon & Schuster, 2016), 526-527.

**Chapter 40: Good Habits**
James Clear, *Atomic Habits* (Penguin Random House, 2018), 17-18.

# BIBLIOGRAPHY

Albom, Mitch. *Tuesdays with Morrie*. Random House, 1997.

Alter, David. *Staying Sharp*. Simon & Schuster, 2016.

Bennett, Roy. *The Light in the Heart*. Copyright by Roy T. Bennett, 2016.

Brooks, Arthur. *From Strength to Strength*. Penguin Random House, 2012.

Buettner, Dan. *The Blue Zones*. National Geographic Society, 2012.

Buettner, Dan. *The Blue Zones of Happiness*. National Geographic Partners, 2017.

Challem, Jack. *Stop Prediabetes Now*. John Wiley & Sons, 2007.

Clear, James. *Atomic Habits*. Penguin Random House, 2018.

Cochell, Perry. *Beating the Midas Curse*. Allegiance Publishing, 2014.

Cohen, Daniel. *What Will They Say About You When You Are Gone?*. Health Communications, 2017.

Collier, Charles. *Wealth in Families*. Harvard University, 2012.

Cousins, Norman. *Anatomy of an Illness as Perceived by the Patient*. Open Road Integrated Media, 1979.

Druck, Ken. *The Real Rules of Life*. Hay House, 2013.

Emmons, Henry. *Staying Sharp*. Simon & Schuster, 2016.

Emmons, Robert. *The Little Book of Gratitude*. Gaia Books, a division of Octopus Publishing Group, 2016.

Fithian, Scott and Todd Fithian. *The Right Side of the Table*. FPA Press, 2007.

Frankl, Viktor. *Man's Search for Meaning*. Beacon Press, 2006.

Frankl, Viktor. *Yes to Life*. Beacon Press, 2020.

Girard, Skye. *The Anti-Anxiety & Stress Management Handbook*. Good Vibes Publishing, 2015.

Hoff, Nick. *Stress-Free for Good*. Draft2Digital, 2019.

Hunninghake, Ron. *Stop Prediabetes Now*. John Wiley & Sons, 2007.

Johnson, Chris. *On Target Living*. John Wiley & Sons, 2013.

Kahneman, Daniel. *Thinking Fast and Slow*. Farrar, Straus, and Giroux, 2011.

Kelly, Mathew. *The Rhythm of Life*. Beacon Publishing, 1999.

Kessler, David. *On Grief and Grieving*. Scribner, 2005.

Krauthammer, Charles. *Things That Matter*. Crown Publishing Group, 2013.

Krauthammer, Charles. *The Point of It All*. Crown Publishing Group, 2018.

Kübler-Ross, Elisabeth. *On Grief and Grieving*. Scribner, 2005.

Kushner, Harold. *When Bad Things Happen to Good People*. Schocken Books, 1981.

Kushner, Harold. *When All You've Ever Wanted Isn't Enough*. Pocket Books, 1986.

Kushner, Harold. *Living a Life That Matters*. First Anchor Books, 2001.

Kushner, Harold. *Nine Essential Things I Learned About Life*. Alfred A. Knopf, 2015.

Lee, Ilchi. *I've Decided to Live 120 Years*. Best Life Media, 2017.

Lugavere, Max. *Genius Foods*. HarperCollins, 2018.

McCloud, Ace. *Laughter Therapy*. Pro Mastery Publishing, 2017.

Mercola, Joseph. *Fat for Fuel*. Hay House, 2017.

Petras, Kathryn and Ross Petras. *Age Doesn't Matter Unless You're a Cheese*. Workman Publishing, 2002.

Sandefer, Jeff. *A Field Guide for the Hero's Journey*. TSGT Publishing, 2012.

Schwartz, Barry. *Practical Wisdom*. Penguin Group, 2011.

Scott, Chris. *The Simple Guide to Nelson Mandela*. TSGT Publishing, 2011.

Sharpe, Kenneth. *Practical Wisdom*. Penguin Group, 2011.

Shrime, Mark. *Solving for Why*. Hachette Book Group, 2022.

Sinclair, David. *Lifespan: Why We Age and Why We Don't Have To*. Atria Books, 2019.

Sirico, Robert. *A Field Guide for the Hero's Journey*. TSGT Publishing, 2012.

Smith, Jennifer. *How to Control Your Emotions*. Self-published, 2020.

Weber, Mark. *The Legacy Spectrum*. Vinton Street Press, 2017.

Weil, Andrew. *Healthy Aging*. Random Books, 2005.

Zeeb, Rodney. *Beating the Midas Curse*. Allegiance Publishing, 2014.

## ACKNOWLEDGMENTS

*No matter what accomplishments you make,*
*somebody helped you.* (Althea Gibson)

I am certainly grateful to all the esteemed authors who influenced me in the process of researching, designing, and creating the content for this book. Their knowledge and wisdom helped enlighten, enrich, and guide me throughout the process. I would also like to particularly acknowledge the important role that The American College of Financial Services had in my education level. In 2022 I received a CAP (Chartered Advisor in Philanthropy) designation from them. It was a subject matter that I was curious about learning more about. In the first of the three courses, the emphasis was on the donor and the why of charitable giving as opposed to the how to give; i.e., the financial tools and techniques of giving. There was an element of philosophy that I found to be stimulating and fascinating. As a result, some of the excerpts and book references in the book came from the supplemental reading material that was part of the curriculum. So thank you, everyone at the American College, for all the magnificent work you do. I received quite a remarkable education, as it was an uplifting experience, and am thankful for that. I can only hope that I have done justice to helping more people understand and act on the importance of purpose and legacy as they go about their everyday lives. Charitable giving is one mechanism to accomplish that.

I have been collecting exceptional quotes from different sources for years. When I find something that I believe is profound, inciteful, or funny, I store it. As you read through the book, I used quite a diversity of historical and contemporary quotes. They came from a number of distinct people from different eras, diverse backgrounds, and contrasting categories. In my opinion, all the quotes and excerpts used in the book on an aggregate level represent some incredible thought leaders. My heartfelt appreciation goes out to everyone who was referenced and quoted. Their clear critical thinking, acumen, pure logic, and common sense brought intelligence, clarity, joy, and laughter to the material.

As in the case of any book, there are others who help considerably in the process behind the scenes. I would like to formally thank the following people who provided valuable constructive feedback, help, and support. I am truly grateful and indebted for their individual and collective contributions. The end product would not have been the same without them. So thank you to Lynne and Larry Leonard, Jan and Tom Tomas, Terri Guercio, Mary Pat Walsh, James Kelly, and Cory Bannester. A special thanks goes out to Robert Genetski, who not only gave me some great feedback from my initial drafts but generously agreed to write the foreword to this book. He is not only a great economist but also a wonderful person. I would also like to thank the professional team at 1106 Design who converted my manuscript into a book. They made the process seamless and provided direction and great advice that added value to the finished product.

Finally, two people supported me from the day I first introduced them to my vision of both the concept and charitable giving aspect of this project. My son Mark and my wife Ruth have been instrumental in pushing this book forward with their honest input, fresh perspectives, love, and kindness. I am eternally grateful to both of them as they inspired me to keep moving forward. I'll summarize my feelings by just saying that I love you both and thank you for helping me finish this book! It would not have happened without their assistance.

# FAVORITE QUOTES AND PERSONAL NOTES

_____

_____

_____

_____

_____

_____

_____

_____

_____

_____

_____

_____

_____

_____

_____

_____

_____

_____

_____

_____

_____

_____

_____

_____

_____

_____

_____

_____

_____

_____

_____

_____

_____

_____

_____

_____

www.ingramcontent.com/pod-product-compliance
Lightning Source LLC
Chambersburg PA
CBHW060900120626
46553CB00001B/152